How to Talk to Christians About Money

W. A. POOVEY

AUGSBURG Publishing House • Minneapolis

Contents

Introduction

How to Talk to Christians About Money grew out of two very different experiences. My 18 years in the parish ministry were spent in American mission congregations during which I was involved in planning and building three church structures, building two parsonages and purchasing a third, and the conversion of Army barracks into a usable worship and education building. In the course of this building spree I was also involved in the issuance and sale of a $100,000 bond issue, besides various other financial programs.

My seminary training had not prepared me for any of this, and I was forced to stumble through various fund-raising schemes, making mistakes and learning as I went. The experience was valuable, but it was also nerve-wracking and troublesome.

As a seminary professor for another 18 years, I was delivered from such mundane things as annual financial drives and building projects. However, in the course of teaching preaching, I developed a class called "Difficult Areas of Preaching" which dealt with such problems as "How to preach on social issues," "How to talk about sex from the pulpit," and "How to present the office of the ministry to the congregation." But each year the part of the course that took first prize for difficulties was "How to preach about money." Students and pastors who enrolled for this class always wrestled with the problem of preaching about money—and often lost the wrestling match.

The chapters which follow are the result of my experiences in these two different areas. The material also reflects what others have said and written about the topic of money. The emphasis in the book is not on preaching but on speaking, since giving is a topic about which both clergy and laity need to speak. Actually the preacher is most vulnerable when he or she is talking about giving since the clerical livelihood is bound up with the church budget. At least the lay person is not under suspicion of trying to feather his or her own nest when mentioning the subject of money.

No complete answers are given in the chapters that follow, no fool-proof program guaranteed to produce golden results. Rather, here are some guidelines for discussion and further study. The "Questions for Thinking" at the end of each chapter are to be used to challenge the individual reader or for group discussion.

The second part of the book contains short addresses on money based on various biblical texts. Obviously the material printed here cannot speak to a specific local situation; that will have to be added. But the 10 messages can serve as devotional and inspirational material for private study. They can serve as resource material for anyone who is involved in speaking about the financial program of the church. Or the messages can be used verbatim, with local references added.

The important thing for all readers of this book to realize is that talking to Christians about money is not only a task but a privilege. It represents an opportunity to serve God and your fellow believers. You do not do it simply because *somebody* has to. And you have the assurance that if God rewards the faithful, and we know he does, there must be a special reward for those who take seriously talking to others about money. God bless you in your speaking.

Part One

The Stewardship of Money

1

The Money Nerve

Edgar Lee Masters, in *The New Spoon River*, entitled one of his poems "The Money Nerve." While this nerve is not described in any book on human anatomy, we all know what the poet means by the term. The money nerve is located in a very sensitive spot, near the pocketbook, and is easily affected by anything that has to do with our cash or possessions. For example, politicians can discuss all kinds of topics without arousing public interest, but when they talk about raising taxes, they've hit the money nerve. Dentists aren't our favorite persons when they drill on our teeth, but the hardest shock they give us is when they hand us the bill. They've hit the money nerve.

But perhaps we are most sensitive about money when we are in church. We all know the church must have money in order to function. Buildings must be built and paid for. Public utilities furnish light and heat to churches only if their bills are remitted promptly. Congregations need Bibles, hymnals, educational materials, and other supplies in order to carry on their programs. Janitors, secretaries, and clergy must receive a living wage if they are to continue to serve. And if the church is to fulfill its task of taking the gospel to all nations, there must be money for missionaries and for struggling churches in other lands. All this is clear to every Christian. Yet no subject causes more trouble in the church than money.

The clergy don't like to preach on the subject. As we will see, they have found a number of ways to mute or dilute all talk about money. Lay leaders are equally gun-shy. Ask someone to give a talk on finances, and it may seem you have asked him or her to volunteer for martyrdom. And the average church member has no eagerness to listen to a discourse on giving. Announce that next Sunday is "Stewardship Sunday" and many may decide this is the time to visit Aunt Mabel who lives 100 miles away. Probably the number one complaint in a congregation is: "The church is always asking for money." Running a close second is the statement: "They never call on me except when they want money." The money nerve of many Christians is extremely alive and sensitive.

Why should this be? Christians aren't perfect, but they aren't stupid and they're not totally selfish. If we are to learn how to talk to Christians on this subject, we need to explore the reasons for this sensitivity about money. Just as doctors want to know the cause of a disease before trying to cure it, we must take a look at the factors which have shaped Christian thinking about money.

Let's begin with Paul's statement to Timothy: "For the love of money is the root of all evils; it is through this craving that some have wandered away from the faith and pierced their hearts with many pangs" (1 Tim. 6:10). Probably the opening words in this translation in the Revised Standard Bible are too sweeping. There are some evils that do not arise from human greed. The Good News Bible (Today's English Version) comes closer to the original: "For the love of money is a source of all kinds of evil. . . ." All kinds of evil is sweeping enough. This statement by Paul should be a guideline to the church.

Unfortunately Christians have never taken Paul's words seriously. The church has directed its attention to sins of the flesh or to evidences of heresy and has not recognized how human beings love money and possessions. John Galbraith put his finger on human priorities when he wrote: "Money

10

is a singular thing. It ranks with love as man's greatest source of joy. And it ranks with death as his greatest source of anxiety." Someone has remarked that the hardest thing to convert is the human pocketbook. This is Satan's last bastion in the human heart.

Paul certainly knew how human beings love money, for he experienced some anxious moments in his career because of this sin. In Ephesus he was involved in a riot let by Demetrius the silversmith because the artisans felt they would lose business if the populace turned to Christianity. In Philippi Paul and Silas were imprisoned because the apostle cast a demon out of a slave girl and that caused financial loss to her owners. In Caesarea Paul was kept in prison by the governor because the ruler hoped for a bribe from his noted prisoner. And perhaps some of the saddest words Paul wrote were to Timothy: "For Demas, in love with this present world, has deserted me" (2 Tim. 4:10). Undoubtedly money or the love of possessions played a part in Demas' action.

We could go on citing Bible passages on the subject, but perhaps a few quotations from the secular world may prove enlightening. Shakespeare has old Shylock say at the end of *The Merchant of Venice:* "You take my life, when you do take the means whereby I live." John Masefield, in a long narrative poem *The Everlasting Mercy,* has a character declare:

O God, the sin
That's done for things there's money in.

Alfred Tennyson, in the section from *In Memoriam* that deals with the old and the new year, writes: "Ring out the narrowing lust of gold." "Narrowing lust of gold" describes the situation exactly.

A humorous sidelight to this topic appeared in a Jack Benny television show. As most people remember, Benny always appeared as a stingy character. In this particular segment, the comedian was stopped by a hold-up man who demanded: "Your money or your life." Benny did one of his famous long pauses, whereupon the robber demanded again: "Your money or your life."

At this, Benny answered indignantly, "I'm thinking it over." The resulting laughter was a little nervous, because few of us would like to face such a choice. Somehow, your money and your life seem permanently intertwined.

Christians may say, "That doesn't apply to us. We have been redeemed by the grace of God, born again by water and the Spirit." That is true, but we dare not fool ourselves into thinking that because of our faith, the love of money has been put behind us completely. The old longing is there. The old barrier against the surrender of everything to God still exists. Our money nerve is still very sensitive, and we often find it hard to be generous. So anyone who talks to Christians about giving must reckon with the power of money in all human lives.

We must also recognize that our modern society has increased the importance of money and thus placed extra pressure on every individual. Money and possessions have become practically the only standard of measurement among human beings. There was a day when great physical strength was the important thing. The man who could hurl a stone farther than his neighbor, the man who could whip all comers in hand-to-hand conflict was top dog. Then standards changed, and ancestry became the mark of superiority. The blueblood ruled the roost and peasants knuckled under to the lord of the castle. That too was put aside, and in many places land ownership became the mark of importance. That was followed by the preeminence of education—the college-trained, the professional person became the object of envy. Today all this has melted into one important standard—How much money do you have? What is the amount in your bank account? How large is your portfolio in stocks and bonds?

Obviously if money determines our standing, it becomes the all-important element. And every time we give some of our wealth, we lose a little prestige. So the importance we attach to money makes it harder for us to surrender any part of it. We want more, not less. Holmes Rolston, in his book *Stewardship in the New Testament Church*, says,

Probably the most deadly idolatry in American life is the tendency of men to become so dominated by a desire for wealth that they cannot yield themselves to love and obedience to God in Christ.

If you want to see this eagerness for money and possessions in operation, just announce a "sale." Promise people 25% off and watch how they will flock for the "bargains." We have become accustomed to thinking about getting more than our money's worth in every transaction, and it is hard to contemplate just giving our money away. Even charities announce that contributions are tax deductible, and often we are promised a chance for a valuable prize if we will give. Thus the gift becomes a gamble or even an investment.

The church runs counter to our basic human instincts when it asks us to give away the very stuff on which modern life is based. The battle between self and God is summed up by the farmer who made a pledge of $550 for a church building fund and then refused to pay. When asked to explain his refusal, he said, "When I made that pledge, I was too religious to look after my own interests." Most Christians seldom find themselves in such a predicament. We all do a good job of looking after our own interests, and that makes appeals for gifts difficult.

But let's not put all the blame on the individual or insist that Christians have supersensitive "money nerves." We mentioned earlier that people criticize the church for always being after money. There is justification for that accusation. In its eagerness for donations, possibly with the best of intentions, the church has often overstepped its bounds. I have real sympathy for the person who says, "No one from the church ever calls on me except when they want money." I think people are often justified in turning a deaf ear to financial appeals. *Church members are sheep to be cared for, not cows to be milked.* John MacArthur, in his book *Giving God's Way*, expresses the feelings of many when he writes:

> We sometimes feel in fact like we're drowning in a flood of giving gimmicks, church stewardship drives and budget promotions ad infinitum, ad nauseum.

Faced with a never-ending campaign to get them to buy tickets for a concert, donate to a bazaar, pay for a dinner, give to a drive for church colleges, and so on, people often have a legitimate gripe against the church.

Moreover, the church at times has displayed a lack of sensitivity and concern for human feelings. Permit me to cite two examples from my own parish experience. My first years in the ministry involved organizing a new congregation in California. When I sat down with my first church council, a rather nondescript crew from my small membership, I asked whether we should use pledge cards for the coming year. One of the councilmen immediately declared if we intended to use pledge cards, he would resign from the council and the church. Since I didn't have any members to spare, that shelved the subject of pledge cards immediately.

Later I went to see this man and asked the reason for his opposition. He told me he had previously belonged to a church of another denomination where members were asked to sign pledges for the building fund. What the signers didn't recognize was the pledge cards were worded like promissory notes, and, when some contributors failed to pay, the church sued. I could understand the man's opposition to pledge cards! I also could have awarded a certain congregation an "F" for stupidity.

Another experience also involved pledging. When serving a new congregation in Memphis, Tennessee, I visited a family that had moved into a house across the street from the parsonage. I welcomed them to the neighborhood and invited them to attend the congregation I was serving. They thanked me politely but told me they were members of another denomination and planned to worship with their own group. Several Sundays later, however, I saw them in church. They continued to attend and finally asked to join. Then they told me of their experience with their own denomination. They went to church and signed the visitor's register. That same day, before they had finished their Sunday dinner, the minister was on their doorstep, asking them to place their membership with his group. He also presented them with a pledge card for promised contributions during the rest of the year. The minister was certainly busy doing his work, but he too deserved an "F" in public relations.

It would be possible to lengthen the list of horror stories. Many ministers and lay people could expand this section with similar cases of poor judgment or poor taste by various groups. The record of the church in raising money is not a spotless one.

Nor is this problem anything new. The Reformation actually started with a quarrel over the sale of indulgences, a tricky little device for raising money. Many dissatisfactions with medieval Christianity arose, not because of doctrine, but because of the greed of the clergy and the unscrupulous methods used to get money from the common people. Chaucer satirizes the efforts of some of the begging monks when he writes about the friar in *The Canterbury Tales:*

> And so, wherever profit might arise,
> Courteous he was and humble in men's eyes.
> For though a widow had no shoes to show
> So pleasant was his In principio
> He always got a farthing ere he went.
> He lived by pickings, it is evident.

The friar has his modern followers.

Now you may insist your local congregation has never carried on a pressure campaign and has always been careful of the feelings of individual givers. That may be true. But churches today are composed of people from varying backgrounds and experiences. In this time of mobility, few remain in one church all their lives. So you don't start from scratch with people; you have to face the good and the bad training people have received elsewhere.

Summary: This chapter has raised a number of problems, but if we are going to talk to Christian people about money, we need to know what we are facing. We must be aware of the existence of the money nerve. We must know how deep-seated is our love of money and understand that the church has often poured acid rather than salve on our money nerve. The result has been that many Christians have shied away from the entire topic of giving. That's not the attitude expressed in the chapters that follow, but we need to know the problem before we suggest the solution.

Questions for Thinking

1. What does money mean to you personally? How would your life be changed if you had twice as much money as you do now?

2. What do you like about your local church's financial program? Has the church ever done anything to raise money that you resented?

3. Is there justice in the complaint that the church is always after money? How do you think the church should meet this accusation?

4. Is it possible for a congregation to have both wealthy and poor people in its membership? How do you bridge the gap between these two groups?

2

To Mute or Dilute

A man rushed into a doctor's office and complained: "Doc, it hurts when I raise my arm."

"Fine," said the doctor. "Don't raise your arm. Next patient." That sounds like a Henny Youngman joke, and it probably is. But it also states the philosophy of many leaders in the church when they're faced with the money nerve. If it hurts when you talk about money, don't do it. Or at least find a way to make the message painless, to anesthetize it, so to speak. *Mute* or *dilute* seems the approach of many. Of course we will not learn how to talk about money by observing bad techniques, yet there *is* value in seeing some of the popular approaches to the subject. In general, three slick schemes have been developed over the years. Let's take a brief look at each one.

1. Total Abstinence. A Methodist minister, the Rev. Hilbert J. Berger, tells of his initial experience at his first congregation. A prominent lay leader took him aside to give him some advice. "We will get along fine if you can preach against card playing, dancing, movies, and alcohol." Then the man added, "You will never need to preach about money in this church." Rev. Berger explains: "I knew what he meant—'Don't ever preach about money.'" That's the principal of *total abstinence*. It is the approach to money used by many churches. Don't talk about it at all. Remain mute at this point.

In typical Christian fashion we have managed to make a virtue of this approach. Church members say with a ring of pride in their voices: "We don't have to talk about money here. The minister preaches the gospel and the people respond with their gifts." The statement seems to imply that churches that talk about money are forced to do so because they haven't preached the gospel as they should. The Rev. Campbell Ferenbach, a Scottish minister, in his book *Preaching Stewardship,* attacks such an attitude rather viciously. He says,

> Never has there been heresy more false and damaging than the sanctimonious highmindedness which finds reference to finance and giving distasteful to the religious feelings and an offence to the spirituality of the church.

Actually the idea of *total abstinence,* of complete silence on the subject of money, is based on the theory of automatic response. The holders of this theory believe that once people have heard the gospel, they will automatically do what is right. It is not necessary to spell out details or particulars. There is only one trouble with such a view—it is totally unbiblical! Nowhere does the Bible say that if you stress the gospel enough, Christians will automatically do what is right. Look at Jesus' words in the Sermon on the Mount. Why all the warnings and injunctions if the gospel alone will do the work? Note the messages of the Epistles. Again and again Paul warns and pleads and instructs his congregations. Read the instructions in 1 Thessalonians 5:12-28. The words sound like a letter from a mother to her son away at college. "Do this! Don't do that!" All unnecessary if people, once they have become Christians, automatically do the right thing.

Perhaps the most striking refutation of the idea of automatic righteousness is the story of the first church council, held at Jerusalem, in Acts 15. The council was called to decide whether Gentiles could be admitted to church fellowship without having to accept circumcision and the Jewish dietary laws. The council agreed that Gentiles could become Christians without first becoming Jews, but the church fathers did ask, among other things, that the Gentiles abstain from "sexual immorality." Such a strange request! Why should they need to be told such a thing if preaching the gospel creates automatic obedience?

Obviously, accepting the gospel *doesn't* assure complete obedience or understanding of God's truth. People must be instructed, guided, led. That's why Jesus, in giving the Great Commission, told his disciples to teach the new converts "to obey everything I have commanded you." And that's why the church cannot ignore the subject of giving any more than it can overlook any other field of conduct. Of course, there is a close connection between preaching the gospel and talking about money. As we will see later, the gospel is at the very heart of the matter. But you can't use the gospel as an excuse to mute all mention of giving. Of course, if a church sets its standards low enough, it may be able to get by without mentioning money. After all, the offering plate speaks on the subject every Sunday. But if Christians are going to learn how to give and to share, they must be taught. Total abstinence is a cowardly answer to the problem caused by the money nerve. We must do better than that.

2. *The Sulphur and Molasses Technique.* In the last century people believed that one's blood became filled with impurities over the winter and so required special treatment each spring. Children were especially vulnerable to this impure blood condition. Purification supposedly could be accomplished by a stiff dose of sulphur and molasses. It must have been a very noxious and unpleasant mixture, but there was some relief in knowing that you only had to take the dose once a year and then had at least 364 days before the treatment would be repeated.

What has all this to do with money? Simply that such a technique is often applied to the subject of giving. Many congregations have as a part of their annual program a special "Stewardship Sunday," usually in the fall of the year, at which time the pastor, a guest speaker, or a dedicated lay person presents a message on giving. This is often followed by an every-member canvass to obtain pledges for the coming year. But usually included with the presentation on Stewardship Sunday is the idea that if everyone will do his or her part, this will be the only emphasis on money during the entire church year. In other words, take your sulphur and molasses this Sunday and we won't mention the unpleasant topic for the next 51 Sundays.

Now there is nothing wrong with a special emphasis on giving at a particular time in the church calendar. We do stress various aspects of Christian truth during the church year. However we don't say, "One sermon or lay speech on 'grace' and then we won't mention the subject again until next year." We don't limit discussion of other aspects of Christian truth to a once-a-year diet. It is difficult for the average church member to grow in understanding a particular truth if it is mentioned only once a year. And if you happen to be unfortunate (or lucky) enough to miss the annual sermon on money, you will get no guidance at all on the subject until another year has passed. The sulphur and molasses technique is an improvement over total abstinence, but it is largely an evasion of an unpleasant task. It will not help produce dedicated and generous Christian giving.

3. *The Dilution Technique.* Have you ever tried to hold a serious conversation with someone about an important matter, only to find the other party juggling so many conversational balls in the air at the same time that nothing ever gets thoroughly discussed? If you have had such an experience, you are aware of the dilution method. Actually, in connection with giving, this method centers on a very respectable word —*stewardship.* Stewardship does not appear in the Bible in the sense it is used in modern church circles, but it is a very handy concept for ecclesiastical purposes. Stewardship usually includes the so-called three Ts—time, talents, and treasure. In recent thinking the term has often been broadened to involve

care of the land, use of natural resources, and all aspects of life where human beings function as stewards, not owners. No one would want to downgrade any element of life included under the term *stewardship.* Certainly each of the primary elements is important for the Christian. We do need to be concerned about the way we use our time in the Lord's service. We do need to recognize that our talents are God-given and must be used in a way pleasing to God. However, the injection of the concept of stewardship into the church's message has often served to dilute the biblical message about money.

It's easy to demonstrate how this works. Suppose you as a lay person have been chosen to give an 18-minute talk on money. You have ample time to deal with the topic and can prepare a proper presentation. But if the topic assigned to you is "Stewardship," you owe *time* and *talents* equal billing and the emphasis on *money* is cut to six minutes. Moreover, knowing the touchiness of people on the subject of money, you may even give that subject less than equal emphasis. In addition, unless you are careful, the listeners may feel they have been offered an option—serve God with time or talents or money. Many people get the idea if they sing in the choir or teach Sunday school, they don't need to give money to the church; they're already doing their part.

Thus the biblical stress on money has been watered down. This is the dilution technique, and it is often used in the church today to soothe or to completely avoid striking the money nerve. It is clever, as are the other techniques. But all of them involve an abdication of duty.

Summary: Giving is important for the church. It is even more important for the individual Christian. The church owes its members a clear statement of how we should use our blessings. It should never mute or dilute God's truth about giving. One of the most stunning examples of boldness on this subject occurs in 1 Corinthians at the beginning of the 16th chapter.

Paul has just finished his magnificent statement about the resurrection, one of the most emotional sections of the Bible. He then begins Chapter 16 with the words: "Now concerning the contribution for the saints. . . ." The great apostle found nothing shameful or beneath his dignity in shifting from the resurrection to the subject of money. He saw no reason to mute or dilute his message. *Neither should we.*

Questions for Thinking

1. How often in the past year has your pastor mentioned money in a sermon? Do you resent it when he or she talks about money?

2. Why do Christians need more than the simple message of the gospel to teach them how to give?

3. What does the word *stewardship* mean to you? Is stewardship largely concerned with money?

4. Suppose a church always has enough money to meet all its needs. Is there any reason to talk about money to such a congregation?

3

Sticks and Carrots

The motorist sat motionless in front of the traffic signal while the light changed from green to yellow to red and back to green again. Finally the traffic officer walked over and demanded: "Mister, don't we have any colors that you like?"

I may seem equally hard to please when, after complaining that we don't talk about money as much as we should in the church, I now proceed to criticize those who *do* talk about money. But the wrong technique is as damaging as no technique, and perhaps it is because Christians have been disgusted with wrong approaches that many have decided to avoid altogether the subject of giving. So let's clear the ground of weeds in this chapter before launching into a positive emphasis on how to talk to Christians about money.

Human beings are usually moved by one of two methods— the stick or the carrot. The terms are quite descriptive. The stick means compulsion, the law. It is the method employed by a parent who says to a child: "If you don't do what I tell you to do, you're going to get a whipping." The stick involves the "thou shalt, thou shalt not" approach usually connected with the Ten Commandments. The carrot technique, on the other hand, is more subtle. It uses a bribe to accomplish its purpose. The mother who says, "If you take your nap and be a good boy, you can have a piece of chocolate cake," is employing the carrot method. This method seeks to move people by promising a reward if the correct action is taken. The two methods are clearly contrasted by a picture of a man riding on a donkey. He beats the donkey with a stick, but at the same time he dangles a bag of oats in front of the beast's nose. The stick and the carrot seem opposites, but they have this in common—both are widely employed by the church in an effort to raise funds and both are wrong approaches to the pocketbook of the Christian.

Let's begin with the stick. Here the speaker seeks to pour shame on the individual for his or her poor record of giving. "Look at the needs we have and then look at what you have been doing. You have money for dozens of luxuries but little for the church. Don't you love the Lord? Is your religion just a sham? You know you can do better! Dig deep and do it now." The message may be hard or soft, but the general approach is the same. The speaker carries a stick. Listen to these words from a church bulletin:

> A church member who insists that he need not support the program of the church but may do with his possessions what he wishes does not belong to the church. He is a disgrace to the church and a hindrance to the witness of the church. He will not be given the "true riches" because he is unfaithful with the "unrighteous mammon." Regardless of what theological interpretation is placed on these words, they make salvation dependent on faithful stewardship.

These words are based on a study of Luke 16:11-12. I can sympathize with the person who wrote them. People *are* stingy with their money when it comes to church giving. The love of money, as previously mentioned, is deep in our souls. And we can always envision a tomorrow when it will be more convenient for us to give and we can be generous with the Lord. A certain man reflected the attitude of all of us. When told that he owed something to the Lord, he replied, "But he's not pressing me like my other creditors." People do postpone, they do withhold, they do exasperate those who are earnestly seeking to do the Lord's business.

The result is that the lay person or minister who faces all this pettiness and greed is tempted to let the congregation have it. If people act like spoiled children, treat them that way. Bawl them out. The law is a good way to let off steam. Many a talk on giving comes from the heart, but it is a heart filled with anger at human parsimoniousness. I can remember a family that aroused my ire every time I visited them. They persisted in telling me that they could not afford to give much to the church because of their poor financial condition. But as I sat and talked to them I could gaze into a liquor cabinet in the next room that was well stocked with expensive supplies for drinking. There were times when I wanted to say, "Stop lying. You know you can do better than you do." Perhaps I should have spoken harshly to them. Yet wrath is not a good basis for teaching good giving habits. As Carl W. Berner Sr. says in *The Power of Pure Stewardship*, "Under no circumstances should a person be driven to a decision which he is not willing or ready to make."

Now let's be honest about it. The law does work. It works in every area of conduct. Scold a child and you will get compliance for a while. Scold a congregation and you will get more money. Tell them they have not done what they should, make quick comparisons with other religious groups that have a better record of giving, and the collection plate will come back a little fatter than usual. The stick *can* produce results.

Moreover, congregations usually don't resent being bawled out. They seem to expect it. This is why people like hell-fire sermons. When preachers or lay speakers take the hide off congregations, they feel they have suffered a little for their sins. And the law often furnishes clear goals which people like. "If everyone will give a dollar more, we'll balance our budget." The words offer a more manageable goal than "Give as the Lord has prospered you." Remember how the Galatians fell back into the law after having enjoyed the freedom of the gospel. This is a constant temptation, particularly in the field of giving. But the use of the stick is wrong. Note the following reasons.

1. The stick always hits the wrong people. Preach sermons or give talks to congregations about their failure to give, and invariably some poor widow will come up and say, "I'm sorry I haven't done what I should. I'll try to do better." Of course you weren't after her. You wanted to hit the old, bald-headed sinner who sat in front of her, but your message bounced off his hard head and struck a different goal. That's the problem. A law speech always hurts the most sensitive of your members and seldom those for whom it was meant.

2. You are caught by the law of diminishing returns. One good dressing-down may stir a congregation. It will increase the offering, as we said before. But the effect decreases if repeated. You remember how devastating it was when your teacher scolded you for the first time. But if she continued to scold, you simply shrugged your shoulders and said, "That's just old Mrs. Jones." The same reaction occurs when we continue to get the stick about our giving. Bertolt Brecht, in *The Threepenny Opera,* has Mr. Peachum say, "Human beings have a frightful capacity for, um, anesthetizing themselves." Then Peachum points out that if we see a man with one arm we are shocked and give him sixpence. The second time we see him, our gift is only threepence, and the third we turn the man over to the police as a beggar. Mark Twain makes the same point when he tells how the preacher's sermon on giving was so eloquent he decided to put five dollars in the collection plate. But as the sermon continued, he cut the amount to two dollars, one dollar, and finally took a quarter *out* of the plate.

This is the problem with the law. It is a tempting method of raising money. It is a quick answer when you need funds desperately. But it is a failure for long-range giving. We have much better appeals than the law, as we shall soon see.

3. It contradicts everything else we say in the church. This third reason to avoid law preaching is the most important.

The great message of the Bible is that God gives. We are recipients of his grace. Of course, there is a certain compulsion implicit in the gospel. God's grace always involves a response. Yet to talk about grace and then to shift to law when we need money is a denial of everything in the Scriptures. As Dr. T. A. Kantonen says in his excellent book *A Theology for Christian Stewardship:* "To flog people to try harder to do better is of course a complete perversion of the gospel." Again he writes: "The greatest danger in stewardship has been the tendency to compromise the gospel through moralism and legalism, drawn from the Old Testament."

Now let's take a look at how speakers employ the carrot when talking about money. We have said that human beings do love money, that this is a weakness for all of us. The carrot method doesn't try to counteract this greediness, it proposes to employ it. If people love money, let's promise them more money if they give to the church. Play on their greed and at the same time extract bigger contributions from them. Get people to bet on God and guarantee them a profit in the operation.

Often tithing or proportionate giving employs this approach. Malachi 3:8-12 is generally quoted to bolster the idea that if you give you will get more in return. What the speakers fail to note is this is a message to the nation of Israel, a message rooted in the Old Testament and one that is not intended to play on greed but to explain to Israel why the nation's hopes have not been realized since their return from captivity.

There are other passages, of course, that show the giver is never the worse because of his gifts. God loves a cheerful giver, and he promises that the liberal soul shall be made fat. (Not exactly the most comforting statement in these days of dieting.) But the emphasis is always on God's grace, not on human beings profiting by their giving. Of course God blesses the giver, although not always in a financial way. And certainly tithing or proportionate giving is a fine guideline for our contributions. But as Bishop Azariah of the Methodist church once said, "We do not give because we want to receive; we give because we have received."

Not long ago a man sued a church for the return of his tithe. He insisted the minister had promised him that if he gave the tithe he would be financially better off at the end of the year, and his bank account had proved that statement was a lie. I don't know what the result of the suit was, but I hope the man won. He had been flimflammed by clerical nonsense.

Summary: Both the stick and the carrot are out of place in appeals to Christians to give, but the carrot is the worse method. The stick may arouse the conscience of an individual, but the carrot only confirms us in our love of possessions. Both methods will raise some money at times. But we have far better appeals to present before Christian congregations. Let's turn to the good things now.

Questions for Thinking

1. Do you resent it when the preacher bawls out the congregation in a sermon? Do you take the message personally?

2. Don't we all need a little scolding from time to time, particularly about money?

3. If the money raised goes to a good cause, does it make any difference how we raise it? Why?

4. Doesn't the Bible promise God will bless us if we are liberal with our gifts? Why not emphasize, then, that giving will make us richer?

4

The Great Giver

The title of this book is *How to Talk to Christians About Money*. The stress is on the word *Christians*. We need to recognize that even in fund raising it makes a real difference whether you are talking to the general public or to believers in Jesus Christ. The techniques are entirely different. That doesn't mean that the unconverted may not respond to charitable appeals. Efforts to raise money for the United Fund in various communities show there are ways to reach the pocketbooks of all kinds of people. The Red Cross, the Cancer Society, the Heart Fund, and other such organizations all gather funds for charitable causes. And some who are not believers put Christians to shame with their generosity.

Also, we are not saying the church should never receive money from those who are not Christians. Early in this century there was a fierce argument in one denomination over so-called tainted money, money that some felt had not been earned in an honorable way and therefore should not be received and used in the church. The expression "tainted money" gave rise to the feeble joke: "It *is* tainted. 'Taint mine and 'taint yours." But the quarrel was a foolish one. Money is neutral; it has no morality. It is difficult to say where a dollar bill has been before it turns up in the collection plate on Sunday morning. A donation from a gangster can be used to send a missionary to a foreign land just as easily as a gift from a poor widow. The question of where we get our money isn't at issue here.

But the church has a special message for the Christian, an emphasis that can't be used with the people of the world. It is this: God is the great giver. He has given his Son for us. He is not a strange foreign ruler who asks tribute money from his subjects. He is a heavenly Father who has given and sacrificed for us. The greatest verse in the Bible dealing with this subject is "For God so loved the world that he *gave* his only Son . . ." (John 3:16). Actually this has always been God's way of doing business. He never asks anything of human beings until he has first blessed them and given them more than they can ever repay. Note how the Ten Commandments begin: "I am the Lord your God, who brought you out of the land of Egypt, out of the house of bondage" (Exod. 20:2). It is only after God has said these words that he asks obedience from the children of Israel. His requests are always based on his having the right to ask because he is the great giver.

So Christian giving is always a response. The motivation for our giving is that we *have* received. This doesn't mean we try to pay God back, for that is an impossibility. It does mean that our giving begins in gratitude. We have been blessed, so we give in thankfulness. An old story on this subject deals with a man who was known for his generosity. When asked whether he was not in danger of beggaring himself through his gifts, he said, "Not at all. I shovel out and God shovels in, and he uses a bigger shovel than I do. And God started the shoveling first." This is the position we are all in as far as giving is concerned.

All money appeals in the church, then, should start at the cross. God gave. Christ died. We have been blessed beyond anything we can repay. The beauty of this approach is that it isn't separated from the gospel but derives its message from the gospel. You don't have to switch to the law or offer bribes. You remind people of the central message of our faith—we have been saved by grace. We have received, and our lives are meant to be responses to what we have received.

Of course the strength of this appeal depends on how much people appreciate what they have received. Unfortunately, many seem to take the grace of God for granted. They have never known what it is to walk in the world totally removed from the presence of God in their lives. Reminding them of God's grace may simply evoke the response, "Yes, yes, we know all that." This is why the convert who enters the church late in life often is the most generous contributor on the roll. He knows what it means to be saved. I can remember a man who joined the first church that I served. He found great joy in his salvation and was a very generous contributor. When I suggested that he might make a good candidate for treasurer, one of the older members demurred: "If you make him treasurer, he'll find out what the rest of us give and will probably cut his contributions." I had to admit there was force in the argument, even though I didn't appreciate the logic of it.

But the answer isn't to find some other motive for giving. Rather we must seek to increase people's appreciation of what it means to be a Christian. We need to stress the positive values of Christianity in contrast to the "lives of quiet desperation" lived by so many people. Too often in our anxiety to convict church members of sin, we make the life of a Christian seem mean and discouraging. It's time we lift our spirits a little, that we say as Paul did, "Rejoice in the Lord always; again I will say, Rejoice" (Phil. 4:4). We need to feel that Christ has delivered us from a terrible burden in our life. John Bunyan, in *The Pilgrim's Progress*, illustrates the blessings of our faith by describing what happened to Christian at the cross.

Up this way therefore did burdened Christian run, but not without great difficulty, because of the load on his back. He ran thus until he came at a place somewhat ascending; and upon that place stood a Cross, and a little below in the bot-

31

tom, a Sepulchre. So I saw in my dream, that just as Christian came up with the Cross, his burden loosed from off his shoulders, and fell from off his back, and began to tumble; and continued to do, till it came to the mouth of the Sepulchre, where it fell in, and I saw it no more.

It is this picture of relief from a burden which we need to stress to all Christians. Obviously this may take time. This is why the use of the law may work faster, but the gospel emphasis makes giving a continuing joy.

But our stress on our relationship to God can go further and deeper. Not only have we been blessed, we have been changed. The Bible says the Christian has undergone a complete change of ownership. When people become believers, they can hang a sign around their necks saying: Under New Management. Paul, in a passage which forbids fornication but which applies to all of life, says, "You are not your own; you were bought with a price" (1 Cor. 6:19-20). He says this even more emphatically in 2 Corinthians 5:14-15:

> For the love of Christ controls us, because we are convinced that one has died for all; therefore all have died. And he died for all, that those who live might live no longer for themselves but for him who for their sake died and was raised.

Peter emphasizes the same truth when he says Christians are a chosen race, a holy nation (1 Peter 2:9-10). And we ought not forget that the word which our Bible usually translates "servants" really means "slaves." We are slaves of Jesus Christ. God owns us.

This concept contradicts the idea that we owe God a certain portion of our wealth and then the rest belongs to us. This is where those who stress tithing or proportional giving often fall into a trap. I remember seeing a religious cartoon which pictured a farmer looking at ten potatoes. He was saying, "One potato for God. Nine for me. Seems fair." But that is nonsense. If we belong to God, so does all that we possess. True Christians don't think in terms of what's theirs and what's God's any more than a husband and wife think about his money, my money, her money, etc. We are God's children. He graciously allows us to use some of his wealth for our needs and for those around us. But it is all a matter of grace.

And still there is more. One of the problems of the "born again" emphasis so popular today is that often people get the idea that they need only make one change and then that's it. That's not the emphasis of the Bible at all. God encourages us to grow, to move from being a newborn Christian to an adult Christian. Peter lays great stress on this idea of growth. In his first epistle he tells his readers: "Like newborn babes, long for the pure spiritual milk, that by it you may grow up to salvation" (1 Peter 2:2). He ends his second letter with the words: "But grow in the grace and knowledge of our Lord and Savior Jesus Christ" (2 Peter 3:18). Paul talks about the Christian life as a race in which we move ever closer to the goal. Jesus himself frequently uses the figure of growth to describe life in the kingdom. The parables are full of this kind of imagery.

Here is a striking illustration that stresses what our life should be like. A man went through an art museum and observed students seeking to copy the masterpieces on the museum walls. Subsequent visits showed him the same students coming day after day and adding to their paintings. They never quite reached the point where they had made a perfect copy, but each day's work was an improvement on what had been done before. The thought struck the man that this is what we are to do in our Christian living. Each day we look at Christ and we try to become more like him. We never reach perfection, but we seek to grow.

Jesus then is our example. He is more than that, of course, but he is the new Adam, the one who has shown us how to live. Again and again he told people, "Follow me." He still calls on people to follow him, and that includes the way we give our gifts. So let's take a quick look at our model.

Ralph C. Chalmers put it well. He said, "We talk about

giving until it hurts. Our Lord gave until he died." I don't think we realize what Christ gave for us. Philippians 2:5-7 places the start of the giving back in eternity:

> Have this mind among yourselves, which is yours in Christ Jesus, who, though he was in the form of God, did not count equality with God a thing to be grasped, but emptied himself, taking the form of a servant, being born in the likeness of men.

That giving was followed by a lifetime on earth, a life during which Jesus did not seek to enrich himself or profit from the powers that he possessed. He instructed people, he healed people, yet he took no pay for any of this. In recent years I have spent time with doctors and in hospitals and am aware of modern medical costs. Even in Jesus' day, people would have paid large sums for healing, yet he sent no one a bill. This is not an indictment of doctors who work hard at difficult tasks. But Jesus could have become a very wealthy man if he had chosen to profit by his ability to heal. Instead he laid all this aside to help others in this world.

We cannot become totally like Jesus in our giving; we don't possess the opportunity or the power. But we can grow to become more like him each day. The difficulty is that too often Christians reach a certain point and then stand still. We are like the man who became a millionaire through successful business dealings. One day several friends were discussing his progress.

Said the one: "Getting rich hasn't changed old George a bit."

"No," agreed the other. "He used to put a dollar in the collection plate, and he still does."

That's the problem. The giver gets into a rut. He or she fails to grow. And stagnation is dangerous in God's kingdom just as it is with water that stands and grows sour.

If we are speaking to Christians about money, then, we need to set before them the challenge to grow. We don't need to expect any overnight miracles. We must take people where

34

they are, and some may be far from the example set by Christ. But the emphasis must be on growing, on becoming more like our Lord each day.

Recently a large denomination, the American Lutheran Church, passed the following resolution as a challenge to its people and its churches to grow:

The Challenge for Growth Giving

... to challenge all members of the American Lutheran Church to increase their giving through the congregation by 1% of their annual income in 1981, and to consider similar growth in percentage giving annually thereafter;

... to challenge the congregations of the ALC to work toward the goal of a 50/50 division in giving to benevolences and to congregational expenses;

... to challenge the congregations to annually increase their support of the ALC work in the amount of 1% of congregational giving;

... to request that General Convention delegates bring word of this action to their respective conferences for discussion and action.

While the figures are purely the decision of this one group and there is nothing sacred about them, the idea of growth giving is certainly in harmony with the stress on Christian living as presented in the Word of God. We need to see such an emphasis not just as a way to increase the budget but as the natural response of the Christian to the grace of God. The Great Giver has blessed us. We should respond.

Summary: The first great area around which Christian appeals for money center is God, the Great Giver. We give because we have received. We give because we belong to God. We increase our giving as we grow in appreciation of God's love and in knowledge of his goodness. These are legitimate and powerful appeals the speaker or preacher should use when speaking to Christian people on the subject of giving.

Questions for Thinking

1. Can we ever repay God for his goodness to us? Why not?

2. Why aren't some Christians truly grateful for God's grace? How about you?

3. Does God want all our money? Can we make a deal with him; so much for church, so much for us?

4. Can all Christians increase their giving each year? What are some reasons for an individual not being able to increase his or her pledge?

5

Help! Help!

"Tell me all you know in 30 seconds," says the wise-cracking character.

"Give me 32 seconds and I'll tell you all we both know," comes the crushing reply.

That's the kind of nonsensical cross-talk that idlers like to engage in, yet the idea of putting something in a nutshell, in 30 seconds if you will, is a common desire among human beings. We want things summed up, put succinctly and clearly. We want no more than ten commandments, three easy steps, one simple paragraph. Even Jesus liked to give his followers and his opponents a short statement of his teachings. So when he was asked about the great commandment, he summed up all the law of God in two clear, brief statements from the Old Testament.

> You shall love the Lord your God with all your heart, and with all your soul, and with all your mind. This is the great and first commandment. And the second is like it, You shall love your neighbor as yourself. On these two commandments depend all the law and the prophets (Matt. 22:37-40).

Very neat. The two statements seem to span all human activity. The first commandment can be diagrammed by an arrow pointing heavenward. We are to love God. The second commandment can be illustrated by a double-headed arrow reaching out horizontally in both directions. All humanity is to be embraced in our love.

Love to God and love to neighbor—two neat file drawers into which we are to put all our activity. Only it doesn't turn out that way. When the Christian begins to talk about love to God, he finds God talking about love to neighbor. The two commandments simply won't stay in separate compartments. God seems to play a dirty trick on us. We want to love him but he won't accept our love unless we also love the grubby, unpleasant people around us. It's like the girl who says to her suitor, "Love me, love my dog." And God makes his demands on a very personal basis. We are to love the man who fell among thieves on the road to Jericho, even though he is a Jew and we are Samaritans. We are to love the hungry, the thirsty, the ragged, the imprisoned. We can't get by with generalities. One of the characters in the Peanuts cartoon says, "I love humanity. It's people that I hate." We may feel like that, but it won't work. That kind of sentiment doesn't pass inspection in heaven.

Moreover, this love for others must involve our use of our possessions. While the commandment consists of words, our response must be a matter of deeds. The man who says, "I feel so sorry for those people who lost everything in the flood," is told, "Feel sorry for them in your pocketbook." Anyone can say pious, sympathetic words, but the real evidence of love for your neighbor is shown when you contribute goods and money to help those in need.

Take a look at a few Scripture passages that form the basis of the above remarks:

> But if any one has the world's goods and sees his brother in need, yet closes his heart against him, how does God's love abide in him? Little children, let us not love in word or speech but in deed and in truth (1 John 3:17-18).

> If a brother or sister is ill-clad and in lack of daily food, and one of you says to them, "Go in peace, be warmed and filled," without giving them the things needed for the body, what does

it profit? So faith by itself, if it has no works, is dead (James 2:15-17).

In both of these passages the response of love to the needs of others is made the very core of faith, the real evidence of our love to God. It would be possible to quote many similar passages, but one section from the gospel of Matthew should be sufficient to establish the point. In his description of the judgment scene, Jesus says he will tell those on the right hand:

I was hungry and you gave me food, I was thirsty and you gave me drink, I was a stranger and you welcomed me, I was naked and you clothed me, I was sick and you visited me, I was in prison and you came to me (Matt. 25:35-36).

Jesus then makes clear the connection between love to God and love to others by declaring, when those on the right ask when they did all these things, "As you did it to one of the least of these my brethren, you did it to me" (v. 40).

Here then we find another area of truth where we have a right to talk about money and possessions and to urge Christian people to give. The Scripture is plain and sharp here. If we love God and love our fellow human beings, we will use our money to help those in need. The vertical arrow toward God and the horizontal arrow toward our fellows in this world are intertwined and interwoven so that you cannot pull them apart. We love God through loving our neighbor. We love our neighbor because we love God. One is reminded of the famous poem "Abou Ben Adem" by Leigh Hunt. Abou is told by an angel that he is not listed as a great lover of God. He then asks humbly that he be listed as one "that loves his fellow-men." The next night Abou finds himself leading the list of those whom love of God has blessed. The two commandments of Jesus are thus closely interrelated.

But to love God by loving the other human beings in this world may seem an impossible task. There are no limits to the cries for help. Jesus' words, "The poor you have with you always" seem like a verdict of despair for those who try to help others. Where do we begin? Where do we stop? It is easy to be like the man in the tale by Stephen Leacock who leaped on his horse "and rode off in all directions." So we must consider some priorities and purposes in our giving. Paul gives us a clear goal when he writes: "So then, as we have opportunity, let us do good to all men, and especially to those who are of the household of faith" (Gal. 6:10).

Those of the household of faith! What a grand concept. The people of God are members of one household, one family. They are our brothers and sisters, our uncles and aunts, our cousins and nephews and nieces. This view of an extended family was very familiar to people in Paul's day and should be a part of our thinking now. If Jesus is our elder brother, then all Christians are related to one another, and we should feel concern if anyone in our group is in need of help.

One of the finest examples of this concern is Paul's desire to help the starving Christians in Jerusalem. He had no real reason to feel close to some of the believers in Jerusalem. They had opposed welcoming him into the church, had suspected him of treachery, had accused him of neglecting his Jewish heritage, and had even followed him on his missionary journeys and had stirred up trouble in some of the churches Paul had founded. But they were still members of the household of faith, and they were in need of help. So we find references in the letters to Galatia, to Corinth, and to Rome regarding a collection Paul was gathering to help out these same troubled believers. Paul meant it when he talked about "the household of faith."

We should also mean it. Somehow we have lost some of this sense of oneness in the church. The stress on nationalism has made Christians in other lands seem like strangers to us. Denominational divisions have made many fellow believers more like rivals than close relatives. And this should not be. Actually we should feel closer to Christians in New Guinea and in Russia than we do to our non-Christian neighbors next

40

door. For we will spend only a brief time with the people next door, but we will spend all eternity with fellow Christians, those who are members of our household.

So when we ask for contributions to help believers who are in need, we should pull no punches. Whether the needy are close to us or live half a world away makes no difference, for we are seeking help for our own. As the Irish say, "There are no strangers, only friends we haven't met yet." That should be our appeal. Someone in our family is hurting. We are asking other members of the household to rally 'round. It's that simple.

Yet this may sound selfish if we don't recognize the sweep of Paul's statement to the Galatians as quoted above. "Let us do good to *all* men" is the appeal. There is a bond among human beings that is even greater than that which ties together members of the household of faith. I do not mean our humanness, important as that may be. But we believe that Jesus Christ died for *all* people. "God so loved the *world* . . . ." So whenever help is needed, we as Christians have reason to respond, for those who need our aid are fellow human beings for whom our Lord gave his life. No matter how far the person may be from what we believe a Christian should be, God loves the sinner and wishes him or her well. We cannot therefore shut the gates of our heart and show concern only for those within our small group. We cannot pray like the man who said, "God bless me and my wife, my son John and his wife, us four and no more." We seek to do good to all people.

When Jesus was asked to define *neighbor,* he picked the most extreme case possible. The Jews and Samaritans were close to one another geographically. They shared some religious beliefs. They probably had some blood ties. But they hated one another with a fierce hatred. Yet it was the Samaritan who stopped and helped the man on the road. The lesson is plain. No other consideration is as important as the need of a fellow human being. And when we add to the story that

Jesus died for both Jew and Samaritan, we have a special reason for asking Christians to help all people.

The most obvious help we can give others is to share with them the gospel. If our Christianity means anything to us, it must also mean life and freedom to others. And we would be totally selfish if, knowing the answer to sin and despair in life, we refused to share it with others. The church recognized from the first that it is under orders from Jesus to take the gospel to all people. The mission outreach is not an extra, it is a must. So there should be no apologies, no hesitation when we make an appeal for money for evangelism, for mission work. When, in the Middle Ages, an effort was made to capture the sacred sites in Palestine through a crusade, people cried out, "God wills it!" Today we may have our doubts about what part God played in that effort. But there is no doubt about the mission program in the church. We can say with complete confidence, "God wills it." We are under orders from our Lord, and Christians can be asked to make sacrifices so that others may learn about Jesus Christ.

But that isn't all. If we are to reflect the love that is a part of our Christian nature, we must be willing to assist people in all their needs. Jesus even said we were to feed our enemies. So the Christian cannot look with indifference on those who are hungry or ill or suffering because of some calamity. We owe this kind of concern to every human being. If an earthquake destroys a village, we do not first inquire whether the people are Lutherans or Methodists or Roman Catholics or even Christians. We help. The church cannot eliminate all the misery in the world, but it can make an effort. We do not need to apologize when we ask for Christians to help the unfortunate of the earth.

Evangelism and charity are not necessarily two different programs, however. Often the only way we can reach people with the gospel is by beginning with their physical problems. Jesus touched many through his power of healing, and the church has followed his example by sending doctors and nurses to our mission stations and by building hospitals to care for many who otherwise would die from lack of care. While we do not desire "rice Christians," there is truth in the cynical words of Bertolt Brecht in *The Threepenny Opera:*

> First feed the face, and then tell right from wrong
> For even honest folk may act like sinners
> Until they've had their customary dinners.

Behind the cynicism we can recognize a truism—if we show no interest in a people's physical needs, it is hard to convince them that we have something worthwhile to share with them about spiritual matters. Jesus indicated this connection when he said, "Let your light so shine before men, that they may see your good works and give glory to your Father who is in heaven" (Matt. 5:16). Thus the arrows we talked about are reversed in mission work. We must reach out in love to others so they may reach out in love to God.

Why all this talk about love to others? Because the church is in a world where human needs are great, where the calls for help seemingly have no end. At times we grow weary and feel like throwing up our hands in despair. But the church should never feel ashamed that its heart is too big, that it loves too much. Perhaps the correct answer is the one given to the man who cried to his pastor: "Must I always keep on giving? Is there no time when I can stop?"

"Of course you can stop," advised the pastor. "When God stops giving, you may stop too." What a wise response.

Summary: The second great area around which Christian appeals for money center is the needs of our fellow human beings. If we love God, we love our brothers and sisters in this world. Our love is directed first to those who are our fellow believers, but it also includes all those for whom Christ died—in other words, everybody. Need for the gospel is linked with need for physical help. We should be bold in our appeals for money for others because this is a basic part of our faith. We love and so we help.

Questions for Thinking

1. Why are there so many poor people in the world? Is God unfair in the way he distributes his gifts?

2. How can we decide who to help? There are so many worthy causes. Which ones do we support?

3. The Christian church began among the poor. Today it seems to appeal largely to the middle class. What has happened?

4. Shouldn't we keep our gifts at home as long as we have needy people in our own town? Why send money to church headquarters or to foreign lands?

6

Open Your Eyes— and Give

The chancel looks different today. There are large pumpkins around the lectern and in front of the altar. Shocks of corn stand against the wall, and there are colored gourds, potatoes, onions, beets, and other vegetables distributed about the church. The occasion is the annual harvest home festival, a time when the congregation gives thanks to God for all the blessings of the earth. The hymns, the scripture readings, the sermon all speak of what we have received from God's benevolent hand during the past year.

Once upon a time the harvest home festival was a common celebration in most American churches. It was a time of rejoicing, a time when farm work was largely completed as far as crops were concerned and preparations were under way for the coming winter. Often large sums were raised for mission and charitable causes at the harvest home festival. Today this celebration is not on the liturgical calendar of most denominations. The service is still conducted by some individual congregations, but it has lost its appeal for most groups.

It isn't hard to see what has happened. As American churches have become more urbanized and as the percentage of the population involved in farming has declined, the idea of a

45

harvest festival has ceased to interest most groups. For those who purchase their groceries at the supermarket, certain products may be in or out of season, but most of us have no real sense of a time of harvest. We do not feel dependent on the weather or the richness of soil or anything in nature. A freeze in Florida may raise the price of California oranges and a drought in the Midwest may make bread prices fluctuate, but that's about as close as most of us come to feeling dependent on God's hand in this world.

Anyone who studies the Old Testament becomes aware that the Jewish people *were* concerned about the harvest. They were constantly reminded they were stewards in this world, dependent on God's bounty for their very existence. And because the people of the Old Testament were largely farmers, it was not hard for them to recognize their dependence. God told them through Haggai: "The silver is mine, and the gold is mine" (2:8). The psalmist struck closer to home when he wrote: "All the animals in the forest are mine and the cattle on thousands of hills" (50:10 TEV). The people were told that God provided the rain and the snow and on occasion withheld the harvest because his people had been disobedient. No doubt people in a rural community today can experience empathy with the people of the Old Testament, but the words have a strange ring to someone who lives in an apartment house in New York or Los Angeles. "Give because God has blessed you with a rich harvest" is not an effective appeal for money anymore.

There are some other problems with this agricultural emphasis. There are years when harvests aren't bountiful, when drought or hail or grasshoppers destroy the crops in an area and an emphasis on God's blessings in nature seems hollow and cynical. In a recent chancel drama I wrote (from *We Sing Your Praise, O Lord*, Augsburg, 1980) based on the hymn "This Is My Father's World," one of the characters, whose home has been destroyed by a tornado, puts the situation like this:

46

It's very simple. If God gets credit for the rocks and trees, he has to take the blame for the tornadoes and earthquakes too. The song says God shines in all that's fair. Well, he didn't shine very brightly when he let that terrible wind blow through here. Dozens of houses hit and lots of people injured. Three people killed. I tell you, I'll never have any confidence again in a God who lets things like that happen.

This is the problem raised by rejoicing when the harvest is good—it makes real rejoicing seem difficult at other times. Since material things come and go, money appeals based on the idea that God has been good to us in material things have a way of coming back to haunt us at other times. This doesn't mean we shouldn't be grateful for material blessings or encourage people to give from the bounty they have received. It does mean this kind of giving has a problem built in. However, if we stress God's blessings to us in Jesus Christ, we never have to back away from that emphasis.

The mention of Christ raises another problem. The harvest home festival has its roots in the Old Testament, not the New. Moreover, it was not unique to Israel. Almost all the nations of antiquity had some kind of celebration to honor the god of the harvest. The Baal worship which plagued Israel for so much of its history was centered in nature worship. And this emphasis has continued down to our present day. To ask for thank offerings because God has blessed us with good crops is not unique to Christianity. Every modern religion can join in such a celebration. To quote Rolston again:

> The danger is that in talking about stewardship the church will think in broad terms of God as owner and man as steward without seeking the unique relationship in which man is set to God in the Christian understanding of redemption. If our thinking concerning stewardship moves merely in the broad realm of a natural theology common to all believers in theism, we shall not have laid the basis for the continuing support of the activities of the Christian church.

This doesn't mean, because others can also use this emphasis, that we cannot speak about God's blessings. It does mean that money appeals based on a bounteous harvest are not too effective today.

Have we come to a dead end? I don't believe so. While most of us aren't engaged in agriculture and thus have little appreciation of how God blesses this earth in times of harvest, we are more aware than ever of the providential care of God. In the last 100 years we have learned more about the earth and the universe in which we live than human beings have known in all the centuries of human history. Science has poked its nose into every corner of our existence. By telescope and microscope we have learned what God meant in Genesis 1:31 when he said his creation was very good. Even human sin has not erased the mark of the great architect, the great artist, the magnificent planner.

Everywhere we turn in God's creation we find cause for thanksgiving. Let's begin with human beings. Hamlet was right when he said, "What a piece of work is a man!" We are truly "fearfully and wonderfully made" (Ps. 139:14 NIV). Just look at our physical nature. Think of the ability of the body to take meat and potatoes and ice cream and whatever else we cram into our stomachs and make bone and blood and flesh from this mixture without any thought on our part. Think of that marvelous computer, the human brain, which can flash impulses to muscles and bones after it has received visual or auditory stimuli. Or observe the human heart, beating about 100,000 times a day. At the end of 24 hours the work done by the heart is equal to moving 12 tons of matter. Or think of—but there's no reason to go on. In the Rogers and Hammerstein musical "Flower Drum Song," one of the characters sings, "A hundred million miracles are happening every day." Each one of us is a walking exhibition of those miracles.

Now turn your eyes to the world around you. Everywhere we find evidences of God's providential care, his wisdom in creation. An anonymous writer has written this verdict: "Man, despite his artistic pretensions, his sophistications and many accomplishments, owes the fact of his existence to a six-inch

48

layer of topsoil and the fact that it rains." See the remarkable power in a single seed, power to explode and grow and multiply. In recent years we have witnessed a great scramble for the coal and oil resources of the earth, yet no human being put a single drop of oil or lump of coal in the earth. God placed them all there for our use. One of the great sections of the Bible dealing with God's providential care is the ending of the Book of Job, beginning with Chapter 38. A small segment will convey the flavor of this material.

> Who has cleft a channel for the torrents of rain,
>   and a way for the thunderbolt,
> to bring rain on a land where no man is,
>   on the desert in which there is no man;
> to satisfy the waste and desolate land,
>   and to make the ground put forth grass?
> Has the rain a father,
>   or who has begotten the drops of dew?
> From whose womb did the ice come forth,
>   and who has given birth to the hoarfrost of heaven?
>   (38:25-29).

But let's move away from the earth itself. Modern science has made us acquainted with the universe in which we live, and the findings have been dramatic and shocking. I once knew an old gentleman who loved to talk about the sun as a great engine, bringing many blessings to human beings. His wife tried to shut him up, probably because she had heard the words so many times, but the old man was right. The sun is an almost unbelievable engine. It is 1,300,000 times larger than the earth. Each second it converts four million tons of hydrogen into more energy than man has used since the beginning of civilization. Blot out the sun and almost immediately all life on earth would disappear. Yet the sun is a small star in comparison to many in the universe.

Perhaps the most astonishing knowledge we have gained in recent years is a glimpse of the size of God's creation. The nearest star to this earth is four and one-third light years away —and light travels 186,000 miles per second! The light we see

coming from the Pole Star left there about the time Shakespeare wrote his plays and has been traveling all that time to
reach the earth. We may shrug our shoulders like the man who
said, "What's to stop it? It's downhill all the way." Yet the
sheer magnitude of the universe is certainly stunning.

For some, the size of God's creation has shattered their
egos completely. The old cardinal in Brecht's play *Galileo*
insists that this earth is the center of all things and he is the
center of God's creation. That was a comforting thought, but
it is one that we can no longer insist on. The earth is a mote in
the universe, revolving around a medium-sized sun on the
edge of one of the millions of galaxies. To some that may seem
humiliating, but to the Christian the size of the universe
makes the gospel story all the more remarkable. God must
really love us if he sent his only Son into this mite of a world
to save us from our sins.

What has all this to do with money? Simply that gratitude
is always a strong motive for giving. We do not have to wait
until harvest time to begin talking about how God has blessed
us. We are surrounded by his blessings. Every breath that we
breathe, every moment we are alive is made possible by the
bounty of our heavenly Father. In one of his rather uncon-
ventional poems E. E. Cummings writes:

> i thank You God for most this amazing
> day: for the leaping greenly spirits of trees
> and a blue true dream of sky; and for everything
> which is natural which is infinite which is yes.

Here then we can approach an individual and ask for gifts
from a grateful heart. If people realize how fortunate we are
to live in God's world, we can stress these blessings at any
time, in any place—at seedtime or harvest, in a city congregation as well as with a rural group. The problem here is to
open the eyes of the congregation to God's blessings. Unfortunately science and religion have been on a collision course
for many years, and the church has not appreciated how sci-

ence has enriched our knowledge of God's world. Few preachers have detailed education in scientific matters. But this is a place where consecrated lay people can be of great help. The Christian doctor can describe the wonders of the human body. The student of astronomy can detail some of the beauties of space. The botanist, the zoologist, and other scientifically trained individuals can be of help.

For the sad part of the story is that we walk through this world never really aware of all the wonders around us. We are oblivious of the hundred million miracles described in the song. Perhaps Christians should take a Sunday off and visit a planetarium or a botanical garden or attend a lecture on anatomy. In his book *Steps to Christian Understanding*, Dr. Herbert Butterfield writes: "Nothing is more important . . . than that we should recover the sense and consciousness of the Providence of God . . . operating in all the details of life, working at every moment, visible in every event."

So perhaps here we can perform a double job. We can open people's eyes to the blessings God gives and open their pocketbooks so they can show their gratitude for those blessings. The old harvest home festival may have little meaning for the church today. But a festival of awareness, an open-your-eyes celebration can reap a great harvest of understanding and of gifts. Paul told the people at Athens that even one of their poets had said about God: "In him we live and move and have our being" (Acts 17:28). If an old Greek poet could write that, perhaps it isn't asking too much that 20th century Christians also believe and respond with their gifts.

Summary: The old stress on God as the giver of the harvest has lost much of its appeal. We cannot ask people to give in thankfulness for a successful growing season. But people today need to be made aware of the wonders of the universe and God's providential provisions and care for his children. So we need to stress God's goodness in every aspect of our lives. This emphasis forms a proper basis for asking thank offerings as an acknowledgment of what we receive every day from God's hand.

Questions for Thinking

1. How does God's care for the universe affect you in your daily life?

2. What are some of the things we take for granted in life but are really the result of God's care? Which do you think is the most important?

3. Can we repay God for his blessings? If not, how can stress on these blessings encourage people to give?

4. How can we make Christians more aware of what God has done and still does for us in this world?

7

Rivalries and Rewards

Carl Berner, in *The Power of Pure Stewardship,* tells about a pastor who insists he has a foolproof way of raising money for the church. The pastor first prepares a list of potential givers and then calls on each individual personally. He says, "When the first name and amount is on the list, it's in the bag. Others will follow like sheep. Their miserliness is overcome by their desire to look good." I do not doubt that this technique is effective, for we are all afraid of lagging behind; we want to do at least as well as our neighbors.

Peer pressure is always an effective way of moving human beings if you're not concerned about the right or wrong of an action. Teenagers, for example, can be moved to engage in conduct that they don't personally like simply because "the gang is doing it." Adults don't show much resistance to pressure either. Dame Fashion wields a powerful arm. Dress lengths go up or down as designers decree. Men change from single- to double-breasted coats and back again, depending on the style of the moment. Even those who seem immune to such changes may simply wish to defy convention rather than wanting to act independently of the opinion of others.

Peer pressure has often been employed by the church to aid its financial campaigns. Many congregations once required annual dues of the members and published a list at the end of each year showing the names of those who had paid and those who had failed to pay. It was amazing how much money flowed into the treasury just before the list was printed; no one wanted to be considered a delinquent. The same sort of approach is sometimes used when statistics are published about congregations. Such lists move church officials to declare: "Our district is sixth in giving this year. Let's try to do better."

All such efforts involve the use of rivalry, of peer pressure, to raise money for the church. Sometimes we even make comparisons with other denominations to spur on our group. "Don't we love the Lord as much as the Baptists, or the Christian Reformed? Why does our giving lag behind them?" Such appeals sound like the efforts made at a high school pep rally. "Let's beat Union High this year. Let's have more people at the game and cheer our team on to victory." When we make rivalry the motivating force for giving, that seems to bypass our love to God and to our neighbor. Moreover, all such comparisons fail to consider the varied resources of individuals and of congregations. We need to remember Jesus told us the widow gave more than all the other contributors although she only put two small coins into the collection plate.

Religious statistics can be entirely misleading. We are never in a position to know what the resources are in any individual case. One Christian may have heavy debts or may be supporting indigent relatives; another may be free of such encumbrances. Comparing their gifts is unfair. Similarly, congregations are not alike. Churches vary in the way they maintain their membership lists, they differ in the amount of training they have been given in the financial area, and so on. All such comparisons run the risk of comparing apples and oranges, and the result isn't fruit salad, but a mess.

Still there is a place for comparisons when speaking about giving. Since few people are impressed by abstract or theoretical statements, the wise speaker or preacher uses concrete examples when trying to explain a point. I used to tell my students in preaching classes they should imagine a man or woman sitting out in the congregation and saying skeptically after each generalization, "For instance." "For instance." We learn from the example of others, and we are moved to act when we see that what is asked is possible.

Now I owe you a "for instance." And the finest one I know is in 2 Corinthians 8 where Paul tells the Corinthians what the Macedonians have done for the special offering the apostle is raising for the poor in Jerusalem. Paul writes with such delicacy, such care, respecting everyone's feelings in the matter. His words are a model for everyone who faces the task of talking to Christians about money. The passage is lengthy, but I will quote the entire section. Try to imagine what your reaction would have been if you had sat at a church service in Corinth and had the following material read to you.

> We want you to know, brethren, about the grace of God which has been shown in the churches of Macedonia, for in a severe test of affliction, their abundance of joy and their extreme poverty have overflowed in a wealth of liberality on their part. For they gave according to their means, as I can testify, and beyond their means, of their own free will, begging us earnestly for the favor of taking part in the relief of the saints—and this, not as we expected, but first they gave themselves to the Lord and to us by the will of God. Accordingly we have urged Titus that as he has already made a beginning, he should also complete among you this gracious work. Now as you excel in everything—in faith, in utterance, in knowledge, in all earnestness, and in your love for us—see that you excel in this gracious work also.
>
> I say this not as a command, but to prove by the earnestness of others that your love also is genuine. For you know the grace of our Lord Jesus Christ, that though he was rich, yet for your sake he became poor, so that by his poverty you might become rich.

That is a masterpiece, a perfect example of how to use comparisons in giving and yet not cause any offense. There is no pressure here, no obvious pressure at least. Paul doesn't swing a whip, he doesn't try to shame the Corinthians into giving, he doesn't try to set up a rivalry and say, "Now, Corinth, let's top the efforts of Macedonia." He simply tells his story, adds some words of praise for the Corinthians, and ends the whole section with a beautiful reference to the sacrifice made by Jesus Christ. Paul knew how to talk to Christians about money.

We can set up a pattern from Paul's words, a pattern showing how to use illustrations that don't offend but aid us in our speaking about giving. The following points are worth noting.

1. Use a fair example. The people in Macedonia are described as poor and having suffered a number of troubles. So no one in Corinth can say, "Why wouldn't they be generous? They had it to give." The example then is fair. Too often speakers select illustrations that are not typical. When the preacher tells me how the apostle Paul sacrificed and traveled and worked for the Lord, I am tempted to reply: "Bully for him. But I'm not the apostle Paul." When someone informs me that Andrew Carnegie gave away millions of dollars to establish public libraries, I am not impressed. He's out of my class. We all try to squirm out of the implication that we should do as well. The illustration must fit us to be valid.

2. Make the comparison a gentle one. Paul tells the Corinthians that they excel in everything—in faith, in utterance, in earnestness, in love. Then he makes his appeal for them to excel also in giving. He doesn't scold. He doesn't make the easy comparison: if the Macedonians with their poverty and trouble could do so well, what's the matter with you Corinthians? The emphasis is positive. It says, "You are doing well. Now let's do a little better." The comparison, then, is not a weapon to use against your audience, but a source of encouragement.

3. Tie the material to the gospel. The example of Jesus is the masterstroke of this appeal. Paul does not isolate Christian giving from Christian truth. There is always a third party involved in all comparisons in the church, for we are first of all followers of Jesus and recipients of his grace. It is easy

56

to find an excuse for human actions, to say the Macedonians did what they did to show off or because they had a few wealthy members, but you cannot argue with the gospel story. Every appeal for giving should remind us of what we have received from the Lord.

So we can use comparisons when speaking about giving. We are not to stir up rivalry but to encourage our hearers to follow the examples of those who have served God through their gifts. Often people are not aware of what can be done until they see what others have accomplished. Comparison, then, can be a useful tool. As the writer of Hebrews says, "And let us consider how to stir up one another to love and good works" (Heb. 10:24).

Now let us look at the subject of rewards. A few chapters ago the use of the carrot in appeals for giving was roundly condemned. To play on people's greed by telling them they will get more if they give more is not a Christian approach to money. Nevertheless, the Bible does contain promises in both Old and New Testaments that the liberal giver will be rewarded. Consider the following passages.

> Honor the Lord with your substance
>   and with the first fruits of all your produce;
> then your barns will be filled with plenty,
>   and your vats will be bursting with wine
> (Prov. 3:9-10).

> One man gives freely, yet grows all the richer;
>   another withholds what he should give,
>   and only suffers want.
> A liberal man will be enriched,
>   and one who waters will himself be watered
> (Prov. 11:24-25).

The point is this: he who sows sparingly will also reap sparingly, and he who sows bountifully will also reap bountifully (2 Cor. 9:6).

> Give, and it will be given to you; good measure, pressed
> down, shaken together, running over, will be put into your lap.
> For the measure you give will be the measure you get back
> (Luke 6:38).

It would be easy to list many similar passages, and these all seem to say the same thing—give and you'll get!

No one can deny that the Bible promises rewards for giving. But this stress on rewards must be properly understood. The passages tell us God is a greater giver than we are. We cannot outgive him, so the one who gives is never the loser by his or her efforts. This doesn't mean we will be richer at the end of the year if we are liberal in our donations, for God does not necessarily reward us with material things. Nevertheless, we will be rewarded. Simon Peter once asked what the disciples would receive for having left everything and followed Jesus. He was told they would receive a hundredfold in this life, houses and brothers and sisters and mothers and children, etc. A literal fulfillment of this would be embarrassing. Yet God does promise we will be rewarded for faithful giving.

But there is a deeper meaning to all this talk of rewards. The truth is that God can only get through to those who are generous to others; the selfish person blocks off the channel to his or her soul. Did you ever try to suck a soda through a straw, only to find that you received just a trickle of liquid? Further investigation showed that the straw was pinched and that was the cause of your failure. When you got a bigger straw, you had no trouble consuming your drink.

That's a picture of our relationship with God and with our fellow human beings. If our outlook toward others is narrow and petty, if we are selfish and squeezed toward others, God can't get through to our lives. Only a little blessing will trickle through. Think of the description of old Scrooge in Charles Dickens' *Christmas Carol:*

> Oh! but he was a tight-fisted hand at the grindstone, Scrooge!
> a squeezing, wrenching, grasping, scraping, clutching, covetous

old sinner! Hard and sharp as flint, from which no steel had ever struck out generous fire; secret, and self-contained, and solitary as an oyster.

It isn't hard to see why no joy or blessing reached Scrooge. He had cut it off by his own hard nature. And the Christian who resembles a Scrooge, even if only slightly, has cut off or narrowed the channels through which God's blessings flow.

So our stress should not be so much on rewards as on letting the goodness of God flow into our lives. We need to open up our hearts to others so God can get into our hearts. God's reward comes to those who are not thinking about rewards but are interested in showing love to others. Jesus has a parable about three men who were entrusted with money by their employer. Two of them invested their funds where the money could be of benefit to others. They were commended and rewarded for their action. One man buried his money in the sand and was rejected because of his narrow outlook.

There is an old story about a wealthy but stingy Christian woman who died, and, despite her stinginess, was received into heaven. When she got there she noticed all the mansions which Jesus promised his followers, but she was given a hovel. When she demanded to know why she had received such treatment, she was told, "We build these mansions out of the material people send ahead of them. This was the best we could do from your earthly life." Of course the story isn't true, but it emphasizes the real message of rewards. God is always ready to bless us abundantly, but his blessings cannot travel over a narrow road. We must love if we would be loved. We must give if we would receive.

Summary: Rivalries and rewards, properly understood, are appeals that can be used when talking to Christians about money. They are not major stresses like God's love for us or the importance of seeking to help our neighbor in need. Nevertheless, we need to show people what others are doing and we need to let everyone know the goodness of God in rewarding those who serve him by serving others.

Questions for Thinking

1. Why do we usually compare ourselves to those we think are worse than we are? And others to those that we believe are better?

2. Paul seemed to flatter the Corinthians. Should we flatter people to win their approval—and gifts?

3. How does your church financial program compare with others in your area? Are there factors that make such a comparison invalid?

4. Doesn't our love of money tempt us to give so we can be rewarded? How can we prevent people from concentrating on the reward?

8

You Can Do It!

A bachelor minister once preached a sermon on "The Beauties of Wedded Life" and felt pleased with himself when he had said "Amen." But two women were heard talking on the way out of church. Said the one: "Did you ever hear a more beautiful sermon on marriage?"

"No," agreed the other. "And did you ever listen to anyone who knew less about the subject?"

That's a danger always faced by a preacher or a writer of religious books. What sounds good in theory may prove to be a failure in actual practice. The material in the previous chapters is only useful if it helps you to show others the importance of real Christian giving. So in this chapter I would like to list some practical steps that may help illumine all that has been said before.

Please study these suggestions carefully, for Christian giving is important, important for the giver and the receiver. It is so important that we must try to make our efforts as effective as possible. And even if we choose the proper appeals, as listed in the previous chapters, we may fall short if we do not present those appeals in the right way. So let's look at a few suggestions.

1. Be convinced of the importance of your appeal. Years ago, on a radio comedy program, there was a character known as Elmer Blurp, the Low-Pressure Salesman. Elmer would knock at a door and then stand back, hoping no one would answer. If a potential customer appeared, the super salesman would exclaim, "You don't want to buy this, I hope, I hope, I hope." And people didn't want to buy it. For we are all impressed by enthusiasm and put off by diffidence. We don't like a *phony* sales pitch, but we do like to feel the one who is talking to us believes what he or she is saying. Enthusiasm is important, and money campaigns have often suffered because of "low-pressure" salesmen.

In fact, lack of enthusiasm is one of the great weaknesses of the church. Ministers present the gospel in the same tone as an announcer uses to tell us the price of potatoes in Chicago last week. Lay people invite others to worship but leave the impression it's going to be a boring experience. But the gospel is *good news*. The church of Jesus Christ is a place for joy, for life, for singing and shouting. And if we believe we have important work to do, if we think the money we are soliciting will prove a blessing to others, we ought to reflect that fact in what we say and the way we say it. If the actors on TV can get all excited about selling a certain kind of soap, we should be able to reflect enthusiasm and joy when we seek gifts for the Lord's work.

2. *Be honest with your hearers*. Raising money is a difficult task. Few people, lay or clergy, view with great joy the prospect of talking to Christians about money. And, as has been said before, Christians aren't too happy to listen. So, let's admit the problem. A speaker disarms the audience by admitting he or she faces difficulties. The minister who tells the congregation, "This text is a hard one to understand and I'm not sure I've grasped it all myself," has won half the battle. People aren't quick to criticize if the speaker has beaten them to the punch.

So if the speech or the sermon is going to be about money, it's wise to say so at the outset, not try to sneak up on people by talking about love and concern and then suddenly confronting them with an appeal for funds. We can be too subtle.

62

The wise speaker will confess that he or she has a certain reluctance to speak about money but the need and the opportunity for helping others has overcome the reluctance. This doesn't contradict what we have said about enthusiasm. It makes the enthusiasm all the greater since we have had to conquer what might have been a barrier to our speaking.

3. Root your message in the Bible. Why are you standing before an individual or a group talking to them about money? You are doing so because of your allegiance to Jesus Christ, because you wish to be obedient to the Word of God. Consequently it is the message of the Bible that should speak to people. Donald Miller, in his book *Fire in Thy Mouth,* says in discussing how to preach on hard texts:

> Little good is to be done if dealing with hard issues should degenerate into a contest of minds between the minister and his people. If however, in the natural course of unfolding the meaning of various passages of scripture from the pulpit these unpleasant questions inevitably open up simply because the Bible has something to say about them, then the offense becomes the offense of the Bible and not that of the minister.

That's good advice for clergy and laity alike. The Bible tells us about God's love for us and what our response should be to that love. The Bible tells us how we are to respond to our neighbor's needs. So our message to others should be grounded in the Bible.

Church members still have a great deal of love and respect for God's Word. They may dismiss the message of a lay person by thinking, "That's what they told him or her to say." They may feel the minister is talking about money because he wants to be sure he will get his salary next year. But Christian people are reluctant to conclude: "The Bible says I should give, but I don't agree with the Bible." So the wise speaker lets the offense, if any, originate with the Scriptures.

I don't mean that you spray scripture passages at your hearers. There are evangelists and speakers today who would go bankrupt if they had to pay royalties for their biblical quotations. One popular evangelist guarantees he will use at least 50 Bible passages in every sermon he preaches. That's just plain silly. A sermon or speech can be biblical even if it doesn't contain a single scripture passage. But when you talk about money, it's important to show people the source of your authority. It isn't enough to show the money is needed, the proposed plans are wise, or the church is asking this of its members. Let God's Word shine, for this lends authority and power to your appeal.

4. Make your appeal personal and human. When dealing with any problem, we try to get an overall picture of the situation. So we gather statistics, facts, and figures about what is needed. We tell an audience how many are suffering from the effects of a flood. We want everyone to know the budget for next year will be $80,425.17. We present a map showing the mission stations of our denomination or the places where the families live who belong to our local congregation. No doubt some of this is useful. But most people are not impressed by statistics. Alistair Cooke said in one of his radio messages to England: "Statistics make few people bleed or weep." And budget figures are deadening and deadly. Numbers in the thousands and millions say little to us. A Lutheran woman said it very succinctly in a letter to her church paper: "Who can love a budget?"

Every reporter knows the picture of one starving child will arouse human concern more quickly than a headline declaring that 500,000 people are affected by famine. Note how personal the gospels are. The writers describe Jesus healing a blind man, talking to a worried Pharisee by night, promising help to a Roman soldier, dining with a small, repentant publican. Once in a while we get a general statement such as this:

That evening, at sundown, they brought to him all who were sick or possessed with demons. And the whole city was gathered together about the door. And he healed many who were

64

sick with various diseases, and cast out many demons; and he would not permit the demons to speak, because they knew him (Mark 1:32-34),

but these are not the passages we remember. We are interested in individuals, not in groups. Lady Glencora, a character in the novel *Can You Forgive Her?* by Anthony Trollope, expresses the human attitude very well.

If I see a hungry woman, I can give her my money; or if she be a sick woman, I can nurse her; or if I hear of a very wicked man, I can hate him; but I cannot take up poverty and crime in the lump.

The point of all this is—let us see needs and challenges in terms of individuals. The budget calls for so much for parish education? Let's see the amount transferred into children in Sunday school and adults in Bible class. The church is giving $5000 a year to help support an old folks home? Fine. But what is that home like? Who are the people who are being served there? The wise speaker will translate dollars into people, into pictures, into concrete situations. We all respond when the truth is presented that way. Jesus did not say, "Your neighbor is anyone who needs your help." He said, "A man was going down from Jerusalem to Jericho, and he fell among robbers, who stripped him and beat him, and departed, leaving him half dead" (Luke 10:30).

5. Remember the importance of education. Jesus believed in education. In the great commission, when he sent his disciples to all nations, he commanded: "Teaching them to observe all that I have commanded you" (Matt. 28:20). Now education is an important task, but it does not happen instantly. That's why the second chapter of this book contained a section opposing the "sulphur and molasses method" of raising money. You can't educate people by giving them one speech or one sermon a year about money. This is a subject that needs to be pursued through sermons and talks and even special classes that seek to teach what the Bible says about our giving. Some Christians may catch the message quickly; others may take a long time before they are moved to real sacrificial giving. Remember, you may have to counteract years of bad teaching or no teaching whatever.

Because education is important, often the best time to present temple talks or to place special stress on what the Bible says about money is in a period when no special needs are being set before the congregation. When the annual budget drive is in progress, the goal is always, "Let's get the money." When the synod or church is staging a special appeal for funds, the pressure for dollars is great. But at other parts of the church year there is time for education, for stressing the Christian approach to the whole subject of giving. We do not want to wear people out with endless talks, but we do need to give church members time to think, to study, to grow.

6. *Take the long-range view.* Closely allied with the previous point is the importance of considering the future, not just the immediate goal. Sometimes we are so intent on accomplishing a specific goal that we weary people and burn them out so that they lose all interest for a while. A writer on preaching tells of a minister who used the example of an old house in his sermon. For the first 10 minutes it was a very effective illustration. But the preacher kept on talking about this old house until, said the writer, there wasn't a person in the congregation who wouldn't have bought the house just to take it off the preacher's hands so he could move on to something else.

This kind of revulsion can occur when we get too involved in a particular financial appeal. Our enthusiasm, which is important, may get the better of us. We must learn when to say "enough" and not weary people with the same old tune. As an example of what can happen, note the great revival campaigns that swept over middle America in the last century. The pleas for sinners to repent were successful for a time, but the pressure used by some speakers was so great that for a long time afterwards whole areas of the country were "burned over." The people had no use for any kind of preaching. In a similar way, high-pressure financial campaigns may raise large sums of money and yet so offend members of the congregation that all such appeals will be failures in the future. The church is a continuing institution, not a one-shot project.

7. *Start where people are.* Christianity is a change of direction, a new birth, a different way of life. But it is also a growth process, and not all people are at the same stage of growth. Some in a congregation are deeply committed Christians, ready to do whatever the Lord asks of them. Others may be tender plants, just getting their roots started. The problem facing the speaker is to get the deeply committed believer to do his or her best without upsetting or discouraging the weak individual.

This is where the challenge of growth giving becomes important. Growth giving says: Raise your sights. Move up from your present level of giving. Set aside at least another 1% of your income next year for the Lord. Thus each individual begins where he or she is, but each one makes some progress. For the great difficulty is that people tend to stand still, waiting for some great event to free them, enabling them to make wonderful gifts. "When my house is paid for," "When we get our children through college," "When I get that expected raise." So the story goes. We must reach people where they are and encourage them to make some movement now. I've had people tell me, "If I had the money, I would give you a thousand dollars for that cause." But that will not feed any starving children. When I was seeking to raise money for a new church, one man told me: "If the last three oil wells I drilled hadn't turned out to be dry holes, I would have built that church for you all by myself." How nice, but that didn't pay any bills. The emphasis must be on "now" and on "let's move." This is the way people will grow, each at their own rate.

8. *Don't underestimate the goodness of your people.* Church leaders are often pictured as visionaries, people whose heads are in the clouds and whose feet do not touch the ground, but often the opposite is true. Our doctrine of sin tends to make us take a dim view of humanity, and we don't expect enough of those to whom we speak. I remember listening to a sermon by a friend of mine one Sunday and, even though he was a good friend, I could have gotten up and choked him before he was finished preaching. For he said to his people: "Wouldn't it be nice if you would do this. But of course you won't." And of course they didn't. He didn't challenge them. He expected nothing and he got it.

I happen to belong to a denomination that has conducted two rather extensive financial campaigns over the past few years. In both instances the amounts raised have exceeded the goals set by rather sizeable sums. Yet the campaigns were begun with much grumbling that even the minimum goals would not be reached. All too often the church hasn't placed a real challenge before its people. We need to remember the simple saying, "Not failure, but low aim is crime." For if we expect much, there is a good chance we will receive much from our people. If we expect little, we may receive even less than that. Goals should be realistic, but we need to have faith in the goodness of Christian people.

9. *Remember the follow-up.* What happens after we have conducted a stewardship campaign, bent on raising a sizeable budget? Often there is dead silence until next year. The committee that worked on the campaign is disbanded, and the whole matter is put back in the file until we need to get started raising next year's budget. That's foolish. If the work has been well done, we need to say so. And if the money gathered is being spent wisely, the congregation should be told what is happening. If a life has been touched through the work of the Sunday school or the contributions to the church's benevolence, that should be noted.

And we need to rejoice. A number of years ago I was present at a conference of pastors and lay people when the chairman announced that a fund-raising campaign conducted by the church-at-large had surpassed its goal. I expected to see the assembled Christians at least stand and sing "Praise God from Whom All Blessings Flow." Instead one man stood and grumbled about the way the campaign had been run, and another insisted the same results could have been achieved with less effort. This was disgraceful. Christians need to rejoice, even in our temporary victories in this life. And if we mean to translate money into help for others and new lives for those who have not heard the gospel, we have great cause to sing and thank God for a successful financial campaign.

10. Pray a lot. When someone is ill, Christians are quick to help through prayer. Most churches these days have prayer chains whose members can be called into action with the dialing of a telephone. This is a good practice, but we should not limit our prayers to the healing of illnesses or to cries for help from troubled members. If we believe in the value of prayer, there is no subject that cannot be brought to our Father's attention. The financial program of a church requires as much prayer as any other activity. When we talk about money, we are seeking to move people to use God's blessings in his service. This is a high task, and we should not be ashamed to bring the entire budget of the church to God's throne.

So every effort made in the area of finance should begin with prayer. The finance committee of a church is not a group of hard-headed bankers planning an assault on the money market of Wall Street, but a group of Christians seeking to influence other believers to serve God with their means. Every meeting, every speech, every individual call should begin with prayer. If our gifts reflect what God has done for us and the help our brothers and sisters need from us, prayer is certainly in place.

Well, there you have 10 suggestions, 10 helps to guide you

in the important business of talking to Christians about money. But perhaps the really important suggestion is contained in the heading for this chapter—*You Can Do It*. The work of raising money for the church is an important and blessed work. It deserves the best efforts of all. The church has been in existence for almost 2000 years, and Christian people have been giving of their means to carry on God's work in the world. Those who speak the truth to their brothers and sisters in Christ have the assurance that their efforts are not in vain. God's people have not failed when approached with God's Word.

There is a story told about a man who became famous as a fund raiser for various colleges. When he was honored at a banquet, the chairman of the group introduced the fund raiser as "The greatest beggar in America." The man rose to reply and said, "I am not a beggar. I have never begged from anyone. But I have given a lot of people opportunities to be of service to their fellows in this world."

That's what a fund raiser does for the church—gives people opportunities to be of service to others. It is a blessed work and, if carried out properly, cannot fail to bless the speaker, the donors, and those who are helped by the gifts of others.

Questions for Thinking

1. If Jesus met with the finance committee of your church, what do you think he would say?

2. Why do we find it hard to talk to others about giving? Is it because we are ashamed of our own contributions?

3. Is there a danger in being too personal, in using a tear-jerker approach? How do we avoid this?

4. How can we keep the members of the congregation aware of their financial responsibilities during the entire year without sounding like we're nagging?

9

The Joy of Giving

It is time for the Sunday morning offering. You can feel the excitement in the congregation as the ushers take the collection plates from the minister. They face the congregation and begin to collect the offerings. The organist plays a lively tune, and the members smile or even laugh as they place their envelopes on the plates. Some people in the rear of the church cannot wait for the ushers to reach them but rush up the aisle and deposit their contributions, laughing and singing as they do this. When everyone has had a chance to contribute, the congregation stands and sings a hymn of praise to God for his blessings while the ushers hurry to the altar and the minister also shouts out thanks to the Lord for the opportunity each one has had to give.

Fantasy? Unfortunately, yes. Christians know an offering will be requested at the morning worship and they are prepared for it, but they don't rejoice over the prospect. Indeed, some place their contributions into the collection plates with great reluctance, as if they were parodying Juliet's words:

Good night, good night! Parting is such sweet sorrow
That I shall say good night till it be morrow.

The only joy that some display when the offering is taken is caused by feeling they are one step closer to the end of the service.

Yet the Bible speaks of giving as an occasion for joy. Thus Paul writes to the Corinthians, "Each one must do as he has made up his mind, not reluctantly nor under compulsion, for God loves a cheerful giver" (2 Cor. 9:7). Some have used that statement to justify their meanness, insisting they can give one dollar more cheerfully than they can give two. But Paul's words should remind us that there is joy in giving, that there is such a person as a cheerful giver.

Again: "A liberal man will be enriched, and one who waters will himself be watered" (Prov. 11:25). The RSV translation is better than the King James here, which speaks of the liberal soul as one who will be made fat, but both versions promise blessings to those who give to others. And such blessings should be a cause for joy. It is the liberal person who finds joy in giving.

The most striking biblical example of joy associated with giving is the churches in Macedonia who took part in the special offering Paul raised for the impoverished Christians in Jerusalem. Paul writes: "For in a severe test of affliction, *their abundance of joy* and their extreme poverty have overflowed in a wealth of liberality on their part" (2 Cor. 8:2). Two verses later the apostle adds regarding the Macedonians: "Begging us earnestly for the *favor* of taking part in the relief of the saints." That's a remarkable witness of joy associated with giving, when the church members even *beg* to be allowed to help.

But the clinching passage on this subject is the statement by Jesus that doesn't appear in the gospels but was apparently well known in the early church. Paul reminds the elders of the church at Ephesus, when they meet him at Miletus: "Remembering the words of the Lord Jesus, how he said 'It is more blessed to give than to receive'" (Acts 20:35). We don't know the occasion when those words were first spoken, but they sound like Jesus. The one who gave his life for us knew it was more blessed to give than receive. He knew the joy of giving, and he sought to pass that truth on to us.

Giving, then, should be a joy. It should be an opportunity that we seize upon eagerly. Perhaps the word *opportunity* says it best, for the Christian should be ready to use every occasion to do good. Some of the joy of giving is described in Dickens' *Christmas Carol* when old Scrooge finally stops thinking about himself and begins to give. Scrooge buys a turkey and sends it to his long-abused clerk, Bob Cratchit. Then Dickens writes:

> The chuckle with which he said this, and the chuckle with which he paid for the turkey, and the chuckle with which he paid for the cab, and the chuckle with which he recompensed the boy, were only to be exceeded by the chuckle with which he sat down breathless in his chair again, and chuckled until he cried.

That's a description of a man having a good time. But for the first time in his life Scrooge is giving, not getting. That explains his glee. And Christians should feel that same joy when they share with others the blessings God has given them.

Yet we must admit, sadly, that joy is seldom our reaction to any appeals for giving. Announcement of a new financial drive is usually greeted with groans and mutterings of "Not again." Christians do give, but too often giving is considered a burden, a duty, part of the cross we must bear because we are believers. And this attitude is most unfortunate. It makes fund raising a task, not a joy. It makes those who dream of better things for their neighbors shiver a little, wondering whether they will be able to get past the defenses of Christians and manage to secure the funds they know are needed for worthy projects. And, most important of all, the resentment shown against money appeals robs the individual giver of the satisfaction and rejoicing that should be his or hers.

What's wrong? Must we abandon any stress on joyful giving? Is that a characteristic only of the ancient church in Macedonia? Let's do a little exploring and see if we can't recapture this sense of joy in our giving.

Most Christians know the word *gospel* means "good news." And it is hard to imagine better news than the message Christ came to bring us. The gospel says God is a forgiving, loving God. It tells us the punishment for our sins has been taken by the Son and we have been freed from all guilt. "For our sake he made him to be sin who knew no sin, so that in him we might become the righteousness of God" (2 Cor. 5:21). The Bible also tells us that all things in this life will work for good to those who trust in God. The Word reminds us that even though we have troubles in this life, there is a better world ahead, an existence where God will wipe away all tears and will dwell with us as his children. If all that isn't good news, then words have no meaning.

Yet in the minds of many, Christianity is a gloomy religion. I once had an instructor who persisted in saying when we complained about some of his assignments: "This is a weary, wicked world, and few of us get out of it alive." A lot of believers seem to reflect that kind of thinking. They concentrate their approach to life on the problem of sin and talk in terms of *duty, law,* and *obligation* rather than in thinking about the blessings we have received. No wonder the world often pictures the Christian as a blue-nosed spoilsport. The portrait is too accurate to be denied.

It isn't hard to see what effect all this has on the joy of giving. If our faith is an obligation, a heavy burden laid on us, giving easily becomes just a part of that burden. If the Christian feels no joy in knowing Christ as Savior, then there will be no joy in giving. So the lack of joy in giving is deep-seated and requires radical surgery. We must open up the whole Christian world to light and joy. We must get hold of that word *celebration* and make it a part of our worship and our living. The old Puritans suspected that if people were enjoying themselves, they must be doing something wrong. We must reverse that and recognize that if people are not enjoying themselves, they have not heard the gospel correctly. For only as we open people to the message of joy can we include

74

giving as a response to that joy. That strange but delightful soul, St. Francis of Assisi, once said, "Let the children of the devil be sad. What are the sons of God but merrymakers."

Chapter 8 of 2 Corinthians contains another significant statement about the people of Macedonia that gives us a clue to the real joy of giving. Paul says about this remarkable group of Christians: "But first they gave themselves to the Lord and to us by the will of God" (v. 5). Those words show us part of the secret of joyful giving. It can only arise when we have cut ourselves loose from dependency on material things.

Permit me to use a personal illustration. I am an individual who, unfortunately, never learned to swim. During my lifetime I've had to stand by the shore and watch others sporting in the water and riding the waves. Sometimes I've sat by a pool and watched braver individuals dive off into the deep end and then frisk about as if God made human beings amphibious. The reason for my staying on the dry land, watching others in the water, is that I've never been willing to let loose and trust myself to the water. I've always held on to the edge of the pool or clutched frantically at the person trying to teach me to swim. And, because of my fears, I've missed a great deal of joy in life.

There is a parallel here to Christian giving. Most people miss the joy because they are still clinging to their money as a source of support. They have not learned to trust themselves to God's care and strength. Most of us, if asked how we know we will be taken care of tomorrow, point to our bank account. "I've got money," we think, not, "God will take care of me." As long as we cling to these tangible supports, we won't experience the joy of giving. It's only when we yield completely to God, only when we trust in his care, that we can feel real joy. The Christian who trusts in God will not worry because he or she has been called on to part with some earthly goods. The believer does not lose any support when giving, for God is the real source of help. In fact, the giver is assured of even greater love because God loves a cheerful giver. If we swim in the sea of God's providence, we will find great joy in giving.

Charles Dietze, in his book entitled *God's Trustees*, tells the story of a person who experienced real joy in sacrifice. A certain young woman wanted to be a missionary and planned her life around that goal. Unfortunately her father died and her mother was an invalid, so the daughter abandoned her plans and went to work to support her mother and herself. Somewhat later, when a financial appeal was made for foreign missions, the young lady gave a large contribution, much larger than her financial status seemed to warrant. The church officials felt this was too much of a sacrifice for her to make and decided to return the contribution. When they faced her with their intentions, she refused to accept the money back. She declared that her gift gave real meaning to her life, for it would make it possible for someone else to serve on the mission field, even though the door was shut for her. She ended the discussion with these words: "You cannot take away from me this one *joy* in my life by refusing to accept my check."

Admittedly this is an exceptional situation, but it isn't hard to see what motivated this young woman's gift. She was giving to something she loved, something she believed in. That, too, is the secret of joyful giving. We may give just because we are asked, or because we feel compelled to follow the crowd. But we find joy when we know the importance of a cause, the greatness of the need. When we think in terms of human beings and not just about dollars and cents, we find joy in what we give. And the more we love our brothers and sisters in this world, the more joy we will experience in helping them. I suspect that was the difference between the priest and Levite and the good Samaritan in the parable that bears his name. The two temple figures had no particular love for those who were not of their class. The good Samaritan seemingly loved everyone, even a hated Jew, so he stopped and helped.

Once again, it is love that makes the difference. And that stresses the importance of careful preparation and thorough information for any appeal to Christians for their gifts. People find joy when they know what they are doing, when they have learned to understand the needs of others. And that joy is increased when they are shown later what was accomplished through their gifts. Blind giving, giving just because the church asks for money, will never bring much joy. The informed giver is, or at least can become, a happy giver.

I've used the illustration of swimming before. Good swimmers know that their pleasure increases as they continue to trust in the power of the water to sustain them. In the same way, Christian joy increases as we continue to make our gifts. The first donations may be hard to make, for the Old Adam or the Old Eve still clusters around our money. But as we trust and as we learn, giving becomes easier and the joy increases. So joy is one of the strong motivations for giving. It is a by-product, but it is an important one. The man or woman who talks to others about money should not miss the appeal. The Lord loves the cheerful giver and the cheerful giver loves the Lord.

Summary: Christian joy should be a part of giving. It is rooted in the good news that we are children of God. It comes only after we have learned to put our trust in God, not in our money. And joy comes when we understand what our gifts can and have done.

Questions for Thinking

1. If a person seems to be giving grudgingly, should we refuse the gift?
2. Why do so many people regard Christianity as a burden rather than a blessing in their lives?

3. Can a believer who has suffered a loss still experience joy in giving? Won't the loss sour the individual's heart?
4. How can we convey to others the real goals of giving? How can we make people see our objectives in terms of lives rather than money?

Part Two

Stewardship
Talks

1

In a Rut?

Text: Philippians 3:13

"You're in a rut!" Nobody likes to hear those words. Ruts speak of boredom, of staleness, of endless repetition. Ruts conjure up a picture of a muddy road and of an automobile imprisoned in deep ditches, forced to travel along the path where others have been before. Ruts aren't very popular.

Yet anyone can get into a rut. Your business life can become a daily routine that almost ceases to have meaning. Your social life can become: Monday, watch TV; Tuesday, go bowling; Wednesday, play bridge; etc, etc. Perhaps the worst description of a rut was given by a lumberman in Maine who is supposed to have complained, "Here it is Saturday, and I've got to go to town and get drunk, and I'm adreadin' it."

Even the best things we do in life can become ruts for us. Going to church is a good habit to cultivate, but if we only go because that's the thing we do on Sunday, that's a rut. Prayer is important for our Christian life, but if we simply mumble some memorized words from time to time, that's a rut. And if we mechanically put the same amount in our church envelope year after year, without any thought of new challenges or new blessings, we're in a rut.

Perhaps you have heard the story of the church member who suddenly inherited a large fortune. Sometime later two of the man's friends were discussing what had happened, and one said, "All that money hasn't changed old Bill one bit."

"No," agreed the other. "He always gave a dollar to the church every Sunday, and he still does." Old Bill was in a rut.

Jesus once said we must become as little children in order to enter the kingdom of God. But he did not mean that we are to remain children in our faith. We are to grow, to understand more, to love more, and to serve more. Every day we receive new blessings from the Lord, and every day we should become more aware of the needs of others. Life doesn't stand still, and neither should the Christian in giving and in love and service. What we did yesterday may have been the extent of our resources yesterday. But today is a new day, and we have a new opportunity to serve and give.

So I would like to ask you to think, for a moment, of the good things that you have received from God during the past year. Let me remind you of a few things you should include in your list. You've lived in a land of freedom. You've been able to come to church and to worship according to your own faith. Millions of people in the world have not had that same privilege. You've had Jesus Christ with you every day, for he promised his disciples and his church, "Lo, I am with you always to the close of the age." When you have fallen short in your life, you've had the assurance of the forgiveness of sins. Even if you have had some sorrows and disappointments in recent months, what a comfort it is to know that God has not forgotten you and that all things will eventually work out for good for those who love the Lord. As the old song has it:

> Count your blessings, name them one by one;
> Count your blessings, see what God has done.

When you do, I'm sure you will see God has not been in a rut. He has blessed you in many ways. God has been with you, always increasing his blessings, or at least your awareness of them.

But I would also like to ask you to look at the world

around you. When you do, some of the sights you will see are not very encouraging. Perhaps our modern communication makes us more aware of the problems of others than we have been in the past. And perhaps there are more people in trouble than ever in the past. Whatever the reason, we can see there are people crying for help everywhere. There are young people caught up in drugs and crime. There are old people who are lonely and ill-cared-for. Earthquakes destroy cities. Floods overwhelm people. Refugees pour across borders. War and hunger strike in all parts of the earth.

But there is even a worse calamity than these. Despite almost 2000 years of church history, there are still people who have not heard the gospel. Indeed, we are in a losing battle against increasing population. The percentage of Christians in the world continues to decline. We are losing the race.

In Lewis Carroll's *Through the Looking Glass,* Alice is told, "Now, here it takes all the running you can do to keep in the same place. If you want to get somewhere else, you must run at least twice as fast as that." That's our problem. We haven't even been running fast enough to stay in the same place. The world's population has gotten ahead of us. We must run faster because the need is greater. We cannot handle today's world with yesterday's gifts. We dare not remain in a rut.

What am I asking you to do? The answer was given very plainly by the apostle Paul when he described his own way of life. He wrote to the Christians at Philippi: "But one thing I do, forgetting what lies behind and straining forward to what lies ahead, I press on toward the goal for the prize of the upward call of God in Christ Jesus" (Phil. 3:13). You see, Paul was not a man to stay in a rut. He put the past behind him and pressed toward a goal. He didn't say, "What was good enough last year should be good enough for this year too." Paul grew in his dedication to God.

That's what I'm asking you to do today. Forget about last year. Forget what you have done in the past. Stop and take a look at the situation you are in today. Have you received more blessings? Do you appreciate your Lord and your church more than you have in the past? If you do, reflect that in your gifts to God.

And while you are taking stock, consider the situation in the world around you. Have you heard the calls for help from all parts of the world? Paul only heard one man from Macedonia speak to him in a dream and say, "Come over to Macedonia and help us" (Acts 16:9). Luke says as a response to this vision: "Immediately we sought to go into Macedonia." Today we can hear hundreds of voices like that, crying for help. Consider carefully whether you can do better for the benevolence program of the church than you have in the past.

"I press toward the goal," says Paul. In financial matters we would call that growth giving, seeking to move out of a rut and to do more than we have in the past. Perhaps you can increase your percentage of giving by 1% more of your income this year than last. Perhaps you can raise your standards even higher. But the important thing is to move forward, to move away from the rut of the past.

Years ago in grade school I had to learn some so-called memory gems. One of them was "Not failure but low aim is crime." Perhaps crime is too strong a word when talking about Christian giving. But low aim is bad aim. Let's move out and move ahead.

2

The Legacy of Love

Text: Acts 9:36-39

Recently I heard a story about a minister who told his congregation one Sunday morning: "Someday every member of this parish will die!" The congregation looked very solemn at these words, except for one man who burst out laughing. When asked the reason for his hilarity, he explained: "I don't belong to this parish."

Small consolation! For every human being, regardless of what parish or church he or she belongs to, must die. Unless our Lord returns in our lifetime, everyone here this morning from the oldest to the youngest will someday have to face the end of life. And not necessarily in that order. Strangely enough, death seems a part of life. All of us will eventually get our names in the newspaper—in the obituary column.

Something else happens when death occurs. We lose all our possessions. Someone else will sit in our favorite chair. Someone else will spend the money in our bank account. Someone else will work at our job and live in our house. As the popular saying puts it: "You can't take it with you." Or in the words of an older expression: "There are no pockets in shrouds."

In Thomas Hardy's novel *The Mayor of Casterbridge,* a neighbor expresses this thought in striking language at the death of the mayor's wife:

Well, poor soul; she's helpless to hinder that or anything now. And all her shining keys will be took from her, and her cupboards opened; and little things a' didn't wish seen, anybody will see; and her wishes and ways will all be as nothing.

It is a solemn thought, but someday our wishes and ways will be as nothing too. Our life on this earth is going to come to an end.

And what will we leave behind? Some of you may leave a large estate of property, stocks, and bonds. Some of you will have little left of this world's goods. But it doesn't make any difference. Whatever remains will be divided up and perhaps fought over by those who remain behind. All you have possessed will be in someone else's hands, and life will go on without you, just as it has done for countless centuries despite the millions and millions of human beings who have lived and died.

But I would like to tell you this morning about someone whose life had a different ending than that. Oh, she couldn't take anything with her anymore than the rest of us, but she left behind something more important than a few earthly trinkets. Her name was Tabitha, or Dorcas, and she appears briefly in the ninth chapter of the book of Acts.

Now there was at Joppa a disciple named Tabitha, which means Dorcas. She was full of good works and acts of charity. In those days she fell sick and died; and when they had washed her, they laid her in an upper room. Since Lydda was near Joppa, the disciples, hearing that Peter was there, sent two men to him entreating him, "Please come to us without delay." So Peter rose and went with them. And when he had come, they took him to the upper room. All the widows stood beside him weeping, and showing tunics and other garments which Dorcas made while she was with them (Acts 9:36-39).

Tunics and other garments which she had made! Can you see that picture? To be a widow in that day was to be condemned to a life of poverty and neglect. But Dorcas had left behind

86

her a legacy of love. She was remembered for what she had done for others. Indeed, her name is still honored in the Christian church, and many congregations still have Dorcas societies, organized to help those in need. Whatever Dorcas possessed became the possessions of others when she died. But the things she had given away—those things remained.

As a footnote to the story, Peter became the agent of the raising of Dorcas from the dead, so she was given a little more time to continue doing her good works. But that doesn't change the real message of this story in Acts. Dorcas is remembered because of what she gave away. She left behind a legacy of love.

The Bible makes a lot of this kind of action. Jesus says we will receive a reward for giving a cup of cold water in his name. And in the description of the last judgment as recorded in Matthew, our Lord tells how he will commend some human beings for feeding him and clothing him and visiting him in prison. When these people on his right hand ask, "When did we do this?" Jesus will reply, "Truly, I say to you, as you did it to one of the least of these my brethren, you did it to me" (Matt. 25:40). Perhaps the most significant passage on this subject occurs in the last book of the Bible.

> And I heard a voice from heaven saying, "Write this: Blessed are the dead who die in the Lord henceforth." "Blessed indeed," says the Spirit, "that they may rest from their labors, for their deeds follow them" (Rev. 14:13).

Now I'm not saying we must do a lot of good works so we can be saved. You cannot buy your way into heaven through charitable acts here on earth. Thank God we are saved by grace, not by our own efforts. But I *am* saying what the Bible says—you cannot take anything with you into the next world except the memory of the good things you have done for others in this life. This record of love is all that remains. Possessions, money, position—all this is of no value. God doesn't care how rich you have been during your time on earth. He is not concerned whether your name is listed in Who's Who, or whether history will at least remember you in a footnote. When life is over, the only real question is— what kind of a legacy of love have you left behind?

And now let's get down to cases. What I am saying this morning sounds solemn and serious. It is meant to be. Suppose you were asked today to total up your life. Suppose the angel of death came to you as in the old English play *Everyman* and demanded a reckoning. You might feel like Everyman, who cried out, "O Death, thou comest when I had thee least in mind." That cry didn't make any difference for Everyman. It will make no difference for you either. The summons will come someday. And what will remain? What kind of legacy of love will remain at the end of your life?

Remember the widows with their tunics and garments. They were evidence of Dorcas' love. And our proof that we love God and our neighbors requires tangible evidence too. Ask yourself: Who will stand up and say, "Look what he or she did for me. Here are the tunics and garments as proof of that love."? And every Christian has the opportunity to leave behind such a legacy. The world is full of places for service. Dorcas found her place, and you and I can find ours too. We may not be able to sew tunics and garments, but there is no shortage of places for service, only a shortage of servants.

Let me list some places for you. We can begin with the benevolent work of the church. When there are earthquakes in some spot on the globe, the church sends help. When there are hungry people to be fed, your church helps feed them. The benevolence funds of the church enable you to aid people who may never know your name in this world but who will rise up in eternity and bear witness that you cared.

And perhaps the greatest work the church does is bringing the gospel to people throughout the world. What could be of greater help to sin-cursed people wherever they are than to be told about Jesus Christ and the newness of life that comes through him? If you have given generously through your church contributions, you will leave a legacy of love. Someone may be a Christian because you cared.

Of course, not all helpful work is done through the church. There was no United Fund, no Red Cross, no Good Will Society in Dorcas' day. Now we have wonderful opportunities to help others through such organizations. A Christian should be careful to ascertain that such groups really do what they claim, for some charitable appeals have become a racket. But the opportunities for service are all around us.

And of course we dare not neglect the chances to be of service to others personally. We may be able to help someone in financial difficulties. We may be able to assist those who are old and need transportation to the church or the store. We may be able to help a young person by words of encouragement or by guidance through a difficult period of growing up.

But enough. You know as well as I do that there are no limits to the amount of good we can do except the limits which we place on our actions or our pocketbook. What I am asking you to do this morning is to remember Dorcas and the witnesses of her love. Remember Dorcas as you make your pledge to the church and as you give your contribution each week. Remember Dorcas as you go about your business every day of your life. Show your love for others whenever you have the opportunity. For some day your life is going to end. When they read your will, your deeds of love may not be recorded there, although you can use some of your blessings to bless others even when death comes. But the important thing is that you leave behind a legacy of love. Make sure the tunics and other garments are there.

3

What Interest Rate Do You Pay?

Texts: Isaiah 5:1-7; Matthew 25:14-30.

God is a farmer who expects a bumper crop from his farm. God is a banker who looks for a good rate of interest from his investments. Do those pictures sound strange to you? Probably so, but they are biblical and true.

The Old Testament prophet Isaiah uses the farmer comparison when he calls Israel and Judah God's vineyard. Isaiah describes in poetic language how carefully God has cared for his vineyard and then voices the plaintive cry: "When I looked for it to yield grapes, why did it yield wild grapes?" (5:4). So that no one will miss his meaning, the prophet describes the situation in plain language:

> For the vineyard of the Lord of hosts
>   is the house of Israel,
> and the men of Judah
>   are his pleasant planting;
> and he looked for justice,
>   but behold, bloodshed;
> for righteousness
>   but behold, a cry! (5:7).

Jesus tells us the kingdom of heaven is like a man who entrusts his money with three servants and then goes on a journey. When he returns, two of the servants have doubled the money they received and are commended for their actions. The third servant, however, has simply buried his money and returns it to the master with no increase in value. This servant is scolded and loses his position because he has been faithless.

Both pictures say the same thing. We belong to God and he expects a return from us. God has saved us, not just so we can go to heaven when we die, but so that we can be a blessing to others. God has invested in us so that we might become what all human beings were originally intended to be—God's children, serving and loving him. And God expects a fair return for his work of saving us.

Now this is a subject that we don't discuss very much in the church. We don't talk about giving something back to God, and the reason for our silence is simple. We don't want to confuse anybody by letting them think they can earn merit in God's sight or that they can save themselves by their own efforts. The Reformation fought against that idea, and it would be foolish to get entangled again in the faith versus works argument. So let me say it as plainly as I know how. You cannot earn Brownie points in God's sight by what you give or what you do. You can't purchase five minutes in eternity with all the cash donations or good conduct medals in the world. "For by grace you have been saved through faith; and this is not your own doing, it is the gift of God" (Eph. 2:8).

But that doesn't cancel out the picture of God as a farmer who expects a good crop or as a banker who looks for a fair return from his investment. The Bible still says we are to be the light of the world and the salt of the earth. It still talks about our growing and serving those around us. Let's take a simple example from an earthly family. Parents bring children into this world. Good parents don't do so because they expect some day to live off of the efforts of their children. They do what they can for their offspring because they love them. But when parents sacrifice so their children may be properly fed and clothed and educated, they do expect the children to make use of the opportunities that have been provided.

The application is obvious. God has brought us into his kingdom. He sent his Son to redeem us and his Holy Spirit to guide us. God has given us a sure Word, the Bible. He has established and preserved for us the church as an instrument to keep his truth alive from generation to generation. God has done all this out of love. He has not sent us a bill for what he has done. But he has a right to expect a return. He has a right to expect us to produce a good crop, to pay a fair return on the great investment he has made in us.

Martin Luther, in his explanation to the second article of the Apostles' Creed, puts this truth very well. After telling how Christ has redeemed us, Luther writes, "All this he has done that I may be his own, live under him in his kingdom, and serve him in everlasting righteousness, innocence, and blessedness." The two words *serve him* tell the story. That's what God expects of us. We are to serve him, to do his bidding. We, by our service, represent the return on God's investment through Christ for us.

Now that service embraces a wide variety of activities. It always means love for our neighbor. It means a willingness to testify to others about our Christian faith. For some it means being faithful parents or obedient children. For others it may include full time work in the church. All these things are part of our return on God's investment.

But the word *investment* conjures up a picture of money, of dividends and capital gains. And it is money that I want to stress this morning. Every Christian knows it takes money to keep alive the work of the church. It takes money to build and maintain a church building, money to provide Sunday school helps and other religious literature, money to pay the salaries of those who work in the local congregation and the church at large. We are also aware that if new churches are to be

92

established here and abroad, we must have money to begin and to carry on such work. The day is past when a person could start out and live off the land while beginning new church work, as the apostle Paul did. If we work abroad, we must train men and women to speak the language of the people we hope to serve. We have to send our missionaries by plane or ship to their new home, and we must maintain them there until the overseas church is strong enough to carry on its own work. Anyone who dreams of running the church without money is a dreamer and a fool.

So here is a place where God expects help from all of us. He might have supported the church by having an angel drop a bag of gold at the church door once a month. God didn't choose to do that. You and I must keep alive the work that has been established for us. And now comes the question. Does God have a good investment in you? What kind of dividends are you paying? If everyone in this congregation contributed in the same proportions as you do, would we be further along or would we have to file for bankruptcy? I don't know the answer to that question, but you do. And I ask you to examine your heart carefully today. Are you a good investment for God?

Please note two things. First, there is no compulsion involved. God gave Israel and Judah a free hand. He provided rules to guide them and sent prophets to help them, but they were free to do their own thing. They chose to fail, but they were not destined to do so. Isaiah pictures God as saying, "And he looked for justice, but behold, bloodshed; for righteousness, but behold, a cry." The same thing is true of the man who buried his money in the sand. That was his decision; the choice was his.

You and I are in the same position. Whether you are a good investment or not depends on you. The church council is not going to tell you what to give. No tax collector from the church is going to seize your property because you have not done your part. There have been times when the church resorted to such actions, but, thank God, such practices are past. The choice is up to you, whether you are a good investment or not.

Also, the return which you make to God depends on your own individual circumstances. Not all the vines in the vineyard produced the same amount of grapes. Each man in the parable was given a different amount of money to invest. God has blessed us in different ways. You cannot compare yourself with your neighbor. The question is: What rate of interest do you pay on God's investment?

Our Bible stories both end on a sad note. Israel and Judah suffered because of their failure. The third man in the parable was cut off from God's grace. I might be tempted to use scare tactics this morning, but it isn't my business to judge you or yours to judge anyone else. Someday we will all stand before God, and he will decide whether we have been good investments. None of us will be judged as perfect, but all will have had a chance to serve.

When William Booth, the founder of the Salvation Army, came to the end of his life, he said, "God has had all there was of William Booth." That's a marvelous epitaph, for it says Booth was a good investment. This morning I ask you to think of yourself as a bond in the bank of heaven. What kind of interest are you paying?

4

This Wonderful World

Text: Psalm 8

Have you ever entered your kitchen only to find it already occupied—by an invasion of ants? I'm afraid that has happened in most households. The tiny insects may be holding a solemn parade around the kitchen sink, or they may already be raiding the sugar bowl or the bread drawer. I'm sure, if this has happened to you, your first reaction was exasperation and anger, followed by a dash for the ant poison to get rid of the invaders. And of course that is a natural reaction. Ants don't belong on the kitchen sink, much less in the sugar bowl or the bread drawer.

But next time it happens, I suggest you first take a closer look at that column of marching ants. I'm sure you will have to admit you are seeing a small miracle. Such tiny creatures, yet they are able to walk, to eat, to reproduce. Ants are capable of performing feats of great physical strength. They run an orderly household, with each member involved in some activity to help promote the success of the anthill. Ants are simply one more example of how remarkable our world is.

Everywhere we turn in nature, we observe evidences of a master planner behind all existence. John Wesley, the founder of the Methodist Church, writes:

The world around us is the mighty volume wherein God has declared himself. Human languages and characters are different in different nations. . . . But the book of nature is written in a universal language. It consists not of words, but things which picture out the Divine perfections.

Ours is an amazing world. Watch a tree leaf out in the spring or survive in a rocky landscape where no life seems possible. Think of a clumsy-looking penguin, a source of laughter, and yet an animal able to live in the frigid polar regions. All members of the entire plant and animal world are capable of adapting themselves to the particular conditions of this earth. How anyone can look at nature and decide it all happened by chance mystifies me. As Gerard Manley Hopkins puts it:

> The world is charged with the grandeur of God,
> It will flame out, like shining from shook foil.

The author of Psalm 8 also was impressed by what he saw in God's world. Remember that this man knew nothing of celestial astronomy. He probably believed the earth was flat and the sun, moon, and stars were part of a fixed, rotating sphere. This man knew nothing of the law of gravity, nothing of the vast reaches of space and the existence of innumerable galaxies. Yet he could declare: "O Lord, our Lord, how majestic is thy name in all the earth!" (v. 1).

The psalmist was also wise enough to know that the masterpiece of God's creation was not some shining part of the cosmos nor some domestic animal like a sheep or an ox. Standing at the head of creation are human beings, and, in contrast to the rest of nature,

> Thou hast made him little less than God,
> and dost crown him with glory and honor.
> Thou hast given him dominion over the works of thy hands;
> thou hast put all things under his feet (vv. 5-6).

I don't want to make you egotistical, but we are remarkable creations. Look around the church this morning. Note how your eyes can distinguish the smallest details here, how they can reproduce in your mind the color and shape of each thing you see. Hold your hand before your face and observe what a remarkable tool it is. Think of what goes on inside of you, without any thought or direction on your part. Your heart beats continually, driving the blood throughout your body. Your digestive organs change meat and potatoes into bone and muscle and blood. What marvelous chemical laboratories we are.

But beyond all this, think of the accomplishments of the human mind. Our brains are computers, more complicated than IBM can build. Human beings can write great poetry, design tremendous bridges, compose beautiful symphonies. God has made us like that, capable of dreaming great dreams and able to make those dreams come true. People who talk of human beings as naked apes simply haven't taken into account the place God has given us in his creation.

The psalmist may not have thought of how gifted we are, but he had sense enough to put the stress where it belonged. He doesn't write, as did the poet Swinburne, "Glory to man in the highest." The author of Psalm 8 brackets his writing with a simple verse, "O Lord, our Lord, how majestic is thy name in all the earth!" It is God who should receive the glory for human abilities and accomplishments. He has given us our skills and talents. And he has provided for us by surrounding human beings with all that they need to exist. If the ground of this earth did not produce food, we would perish. If the rain didn't fall, human life would soon die out. If God had not put minerals in the soil, our technological civilization would never have come into being. We are residents on Spaceship Earth, but if God hadn't packed the earth full of supplies, we would have perished long ago.

And now I want to add two truths to this psalm. The writer did not know or think of everything when he penned his beautiful words. He did not know, first of all, that God has redeemed us in Jesus Christ. The words of Psalm 8 were written B.C., not A.D. We have evidence of God's grace and his providential care of us that reaches beyond the physical world, beyond the powers of our own brain. We know of a God who loves us so much that he gave his own Son for our salvation. We have more reason than the psalmist for saying, "O Lord, our Lord, how majestic is thy name in all the earth!"

The psalmist begins and ends his song with those words of praise. I would not fault him for that. But I believe that today we can add a message of gratitude, a response to all God's goodness. If God has been so good to us, through creation and redemption, is it asking too much that we show our gratitude through our prayers and our gifts? Each time we experience some part of God's creation, but particularly when we remember what we have received in Jesus Christ, our hearts should be filled with gratitude.

Of course you cannot pay God for what you have received. We cannot repay him for the beautiful sunset or the stars that twinkle at night. We cannot pay God for our steady heartbeat any more than we can pay for the redemption we have received in Christ. But we can be grateful, and we can show our gratitude by the gifts we make to God's work. Every breath that we take, every bit of food we eat or water we drink, comes to us from the hands of a loving God. Is it asking too much to be called on to share with others some of the money we have as a result of God's blessing?

There was a day when we had a harvest home festival in the church to show our thanks for the bumper crop received each fall. That practice has fallen into disuse in most parts of the church today. Actually, however, we have cause to hold a harvest festival every Sunday. For we are always receiving blessings from God. I ask you this morning, then, to join the psalmist in saying, "O Lord, our Lord, how majestic is thy name in all the earth!" And then I ask you to respond to those words by bringing your gifts in gratitude to the Lord.

5

Now! Now! Now!

I am sure that almost everyone here this morning has, at some time, made a New Year's resolution. I am equally sure that most of us have failed to keep that resolution. Somehow our good intentions seem to fade away as the year moves on. It is discouraging to make a fine resolution and then fail to keep it. But our human ingenuity usually comes to our aid. We decide that we didn't break our resolve, we just postponed it.

You know how it goes. Dieting is a good idea, but I'll do it a little later on. I should quit smoking, and I will, but not just now when I'm under a lot of tension. Reading the Bible every day is the proper thing for a Christian, but I'll postpone my reading until I'm not quite so busy. That's the way, isn't it? We are good at drafting resolutions, but we are even better at finding reasons for postponing action. We are procrastinators, to give the practice a fancy name.

But procrastination is a dangerous game to play. Jesus warned against it when he told his disciples: "We must work the works of him who sent me, while it is day; night comes, when no one can work" (John 9:4). In other words, Jesus told his followers that we have *now*, but we don't know anything about *after*. Today is here, but we know nothing about tomorrow.

Jesus' words can apply to every aspect of our lives, but I'm interested this morning in stressing the "now" in connection with our giving. For this is the place where we are most tempted to postpone, to procrastinate. We are sure we will be able to give more to the church when we get a few bills paid. We intend to increase our contributions just as soon as we get our children through college. We give priority to a dozen other obligations. We feel like the man who was reminded that he owed God something for the many blessings he had received. "Yes," he said, "but God's not pressing me like my other creditors are."

I'm reminded of a certain young man who was asked by an anxious father what his intentions were toward the young lady whom he was courting. The suitor replied: "My intentions are honorable but remote." That's a very easy attitude to adopt, but Jesus warns us we can't play that kind of game with God. Our intentions dare not be remote. We must work while it is day, for the night is hurrying toward us.

There are two simple reasons why we should make our contributions now. The first is, the need is now. When the church asks for money, it does so because it senses a need. And because there are so many places to serve, the church can never lay aside funds for a rainy day. We must help when people need help, and that's a situation that never changes. So we need to give now as well as later.

Suppose a tornado struck a section of our community and left many people homeless. There would be an immediate call for funds to help the unfortunate. Which one of us would say, "I will be glad to give. Please come and see me next year. I'll be in better financial shape then."? We wouldn't even attempt such a silly answer. People without a home need help immediately. Next year may be too late.

All the appeals of the church are like that. If people are hungry, they need to be fed now. If people are in trouble and need counseling, they need it now. If people have not heard the gospel, the time to bring it to them is now. Whether we are concerned about physical or spiritual needs, the call to us is to do good while it is day, for the night keeps coming for the people of the world. Frustration, disillusionment, and death are always at work. People are being plunged into eternity without the gospel because no one has told them about God's gift of his Son. Tomorrow may be too late.

An Eskimo, upon hearing the gospel, demanded to know: "How long have you white people known about Jesus as Savior?" When told that the gospel had been known for centuries, the Eskimo then asked: "What took you so long getting here with the message?" There is no answer to that except that we have postponed action too much in the past. The night has come for too many people while we have waited for a more favorable time.

The message of the Bible, then, is very clear. If we are going to help the people of this world, we must do it now. Tomorrow may be too late. The people may not be there, or their condition may have so deteriorated that they no longer can be helped. Our action and our gifts must be given now.

But I said there were two reasons why we must heed Jesus' words. The second one is as simple as the first. The people needing help may still be waiting tomorrow, but you may not be any more able to help. The idea that next year will be a better time for you to give or to serve rests on a false assumption. You don't know anything about next year, or even next week. Sometimes preachers use this passage of Scripture to try to scare people into doing better. I don't want to scare anyone. I simply ask you to look around you this morning and to try to remember all the people who have worshiped with you during the past 10 years. Some of them are not here anymore, are they? The night has come for them. They have lost the chance to be of service to others.

Charles Dickens has a particularly touching scene in his famous *Christmas Carol.* He pictures a number of ghosts floating in the air, trying to help some human beings below. But they can do nothing. Their time of service has come to an end. And you and I can take that lesson to heart. We can help now, but there will come a time when our opportunities will be gone.

I'm aware that we don't like to hear this. We like to think that time stands still, that tomorrow will be just the same as today. We fool ourselves by telling each other we look just as young as we ever did. But that's not true. The 15-year-old is not as young as he or she was one year ago. The 45-year-old man is five years older than he was at 40, and no compliments or face-lifts can conceal that fact. The English poet Andrew Marvell wrote two immortal lines in a love poem "To His Coy Mistress":

But at my back I always hear
Time's winged chariot hurrying near.

That's the problem we face. Time's winged chariot is always hurrying near, pushing us closer to the night, when no one can work.

So let's be honest about it. If we intend to give anything for God's work, the time is now. If we intend to serve, the time is now. That doesn't mean you may not be alive to serve and give next year or 10 years from now. It only means that as Christians we are to live in the present.

I once heard a comedian say we should live each day as if it were our last, and someday we will be right. That's a witty remark, but it is also the truth. The emphasis in God's Word is on that simple three-letter word—*now*.

Jaroslav J. Vajda has written a beautiful hymn that stresses the presence of God in the communion service. The hymn begins with the words: "Now the silence, now the peace," and moves on to stress that now is the time for kneeling, for power, for body, for blood, and so on. The hymn ends with three words, "Now. Now. Now."

102

It is a beautiful communion hymn, but I wish there were more verses to it, verses that would stress that now is the time to help our brothers and sisters in this life, that now is the time to give and to serve, that now is the time to live like a Christian, for the night comes when no one can work.

6

Everything She Had

Text: Mark 12:41-44

Some passages in the Bible make us nervous. When we hear them, we immediately begin to wonder how they apply to us and whether they are intended to restrict our pleasures. The story of the poor widow who deposited two small coins in the temple treasury in Jerusalem is one of those "nervous" passages.

You remember the story? Jesus is in the temple at Jerusalem and he sits there watching people make their contributions to the treasury. He sees rich people placing large sums of money into the collection box. Then along comes a poor widow who gives only two small coins, but Jesus tells his disciples that this woman has given more than any of the others, for she gave everything she had.

That's where the story makes us nervous. Are we expected to be like that widow? Am I going to tell you this morning that if you want to please Jesus, you must give all your money to the church? I can see some of you getting your defenses ready. You're going to tell me you will consider making such a sacrifice, but I must lead the way. "After you," you will say politely.

You can relax. I don't believe Jesus asks his followers to give all their money away. He only demanded such a sacrifice from one man, the rich young ruler, and that was a case of major surgery being necessary to save the man's spiritual life. Jesus makes his point when he declares the widow gave more than the rest because she gave out of her poverty, she put in everything she had.

But there is a deeper meaning here too, a meaning that centers around the widow and her motive for this splendid gift. We don't know this woman's name. We don't know anything else about her, for she appears in the Bible only in this brief episode. Yet certain truths follow from the strange action this widow took.

She gave all she had. That was an extraordinary thing for a widow to do. As one writer has put it, she didn't tithe—she *totaled.* She gave only two small coins, but that was the extent of her earthly goods.

How could she do such a thing? Some male chauvinists are inclined to say, "It just shows. Women don't know how to handle money. It was a silly, sentimental thing to do." But Jesus is never inclined to be silly or sentimental or to commend such actions in others. The explanation for the widow's action is very simple: she trusted in God.

She didn't feel she was doing something rash. She had no intention of starving herself to death through her generosity. She gave, but she knew someone who gave even more generously—her heavenly Father. God would take care of her needs.

Isn't that what the Bible says? Think of the beautiful beginning to the 23rd Psalm: "The Lord is my shepherd, I shall not want." Later in the psalms we read: "I have been young, and now am old; yet I have not seen the righteous forsaken or his children begging bread" (Ps. 37:25). And perhaps the most sweeping statement on this subject is Jesus' declaration in the the Sermon on the Mount:

Therefore I tell you, do not be anxious about your life, what you shall eat or what you shall drink, nor about your body, what you shall put on. Is not life more than food, and the body more than clothing? Look at the birds of the air: they neither sow nor reap nor gather into barns, and yet your heavenly Father feeds them. Are you not of more value than they? (Matt. 6:25-26).

This is where true giving starts—with trust in God. This is not a matter of amounts, but of life-style. If we think our protection in life resides in our bank account, then giving is simply tossing God a tip, no matter how much we give. But if we trust in God, if we have committed our lives to him, then our gifts become a measure of our trust.

This is why the Bible seems to condemn the rich and to warn against accumulated wealth. Having money is not a sin, but it is a temptation. It tempts us to put our trust in what we have rather than in God. Those rich people who gave large sums to the temple treasury gave out of their abundance, said Jesus. They may have also trusted in God. We don't know. But the widow *had* to trust when she made her gift. She had no other place to turn.

Of course, such faith doesn't suddenly blossom forth. It is something that grows through years of finding that God keeps his word. It's like walking on ice across a lake. You begin very cautiously, creeping forward and testing every inch of the way. But when you realize the ice is strong, you walk across it confidently. So we grow as we trust and find our trust is not misplaced. We learn to give and not to worry about tomorrow.

But I believe we can say something else about the actions of this poor widow. What she did also came from love. No law forced her to give. If she had kept her money, no one would have been the wiser, and the temple treasury would have suffered only a very small loss. But she gave. You don't part with your last penny except for someone you love, someone you feel very near to. The widow must have loved God, otherwise she would never have made such a sacrifice. And we marvel at that love. She was a woman, and in her day women occupied a very inferior place in worship. She could only go to a certain point in the temple. Beyond the court of the women was the place where the men gathered. Then there was an area for the priests, and beyond that there was a holy place open only to the high priest once a year. God must have seemed rather remote to this widow, yet she loved him and remembered to worship him.

Think what our situation is in comparison to this woman. We have complete access to God. No human priest intervenes. No ritual laws bind us. We have a Savior who has come from God and has paid the penalty for our sins. We live in the New Testament world where God has fulfilled the promises he made long ago to his people. There is a rather melancholy passage at the end of Hebrews 11 where the author, after listing all the great saints of the Old Testament, says, "And all these, though well attested by their faith, did not receive what was promised, since God had foreseen something better for us, that apart from us they should not be made perfect" (vv. 39-40). This woman lived in the same situation, yet she loved so much that she gave everything she had.

Love and trust! Such beautiful words. Those words explain why this poor widow could give the church such a powerful lesson in giving. And they teach us how our giving should be. I said at the beginning of this talk I wasn't going to ask you to give everything you have to the church. I intend to keep that promise. No one says you must give everything you have, as this woman did, in order to be a faithful Christian. But I think God does ask you to give in the same way the widow did—in love and trust. It is not a matter of amount, it is a matter of attitude.

So, as you make your pledges and bring your offerings, I ask you to begin by putting your trust in God to care for you as he has in the past. I ask you to remember how good God has been to you and then, in a response of love, to give to God's work.

There is one interesting sidelight that I must still mention.

The story of the widow's mite begins with Jesus sitting opposite the treasury, observing what people were donating. I think we have a similar situation here today. Jesus is here, for he promises to be with any who gather in his name. He is here and he sees in your heart what motivates your giving. He knows your intentions and he knows whether you are making a sacrificial gift to the Lord. This is not a matter between you and me or between you and the church; it's between you and the Lord. So it's up to you. You must take it from there.

7

An Exchange of Gifts

Text: John 3:16

Every Christian has heard John 3:16. Many know it by heart. "For God so loved the world that he gave his only Son, that whoever believes in him should not perish but have eternal life." This is one of the most quoted verses of Scripture. John 3:16 has been called "the gospel in miniature," and it *is* a clear statement of the basic beliefs confessed by Christians. Yet even in this short statement there are some truths that have been overlooked or slighted. This morning I would like to concentrate on one four-letter word—*gave*. God *gave* his only Son.

It's easy to hop over that simple verb. We note that John tells us God loved this world. We concentrate our thinking on the Son, Jesus Christ, and then we hurry on to the part of the verse that reminds us if we believe, we will not perish but have eternal life. But the fact that all this was a gift from God, that he *gave*, doesn't get its proper stress. Yet the emphasis on God as the giver is vital to understanding everything in the Bible.

Note how Scripture begins: "In the beginning God created the heavens and the earth." We had nothing to do with it. Human beings weren't even in existence. God gave the whole universe its existence. The initiative was with him. His first gift was this world. And every step along the way follows the same pattern. The divine action always comes first. It was God who warned Noah of the flood and instructed him how to prepare his escape. It was God who ordered Abraham to move to the promised land and who told him his descendants would be a blessing to the whole world. It was God who called Moses to lead Israel out of Egypt and out of captivity. God was always the giver. The initiative was always with him.

It is interesting to note that the New Testament follows the same pattern. God again gives. He sends an angel to Mary to tell her she is to bear a son who will save his people from their sins. Mary didn't plan any of this herself. Once again the initiative was with God. He gave. I think this stresses the importance of the Virgin Birth. It was not necessary to have Jesus born of a virgin so he would be sinless. God could have accomplished that in some other fashion. But the Virgin Birth again shows God acting, God as the giver.

Now why do I make such a point of all this theology? Because I'm talking about *our* giving this morning, and it is vital for us to understand that all our giving is a reaction to what God has done. Nowhere is God portrayed as one who approaches us with a tin cup, saying, "Won't you spare a few coins for my work?" God is always the first giver, the one who has already acted, and when we give we are only reacting to his love.

Observe how the Ten Commandments begin. We usually think of the commandments as stern rules God has handed to us, like a municipal council setting down rules for conduct in the town. But Exodus 20:2 reads: "I am the Lord your God, who brought you out of the land of Egypt, out of the house of bondage." It is only after those words, reminding Israel of God's goodness to them, that the Lord says, "You shall have no other gods before me," etc. God always blesses us first. Then he calls on us to respond.

God, then, is like the mother in the old story about the boy who wanted to be paid for everything he did. The boy decided to present a bill to his mother for all the chores he was performing. The bill read like this:

$5.00 each week for mowing the grass
$1.00 for each trip made to the store
$1.00 for closing the garage door
each time you back the car out.
Etc., etc.

The mother wisely did not argue with her son. She simply made out a bill for him too. It read like this:

$1000 for bringing you into the world
$100 for feeding you
until you were able to feed yourself
$200 for teaching you to walk and to talk
Etc., etc.

The boy didn't send any more bills. He realized he would always remain in debt to those who loved him.

In the same way, God is the first giver. And because that is so, I can speak with a clear conscience this morning when I ask you to give to the church in order to carry on God's work in the world. I am not begging this morning. I am not demanding. I'm simply reminding you that you have already been blessed. God has been busy giving to you. All I am asking, therefore, is a response to his goodness.

And what a contrast in the gifts involved. Did you ever get a Christmas present from a friend or relative and then do a little comparing? "Why, that gift I sent him must have been worth five times this thing he sent me. I certainly got cheated in this exchange of gifts." Of course God isn't going to treat your contribution like that. Still, a bit of comparing might be interesting.

What did God give for us, according to John 3:16? His only Son. The Bible is rather quiet about that gift. It does speak of Jesus laying aside his place in heaven and taking upon himself the yoke of humanity. John later tells us of the suffering of

Jesus so that we might be forgiven. But we are not told of God the Father's reaction, except in the way the terms *father* and *son* speak to us.

There is a memorable scene at the end of the play *Green Pastures* that seeks to penetrate the mystery a bit. The playwright, who tells his story through the eyes of simple black people, shows God sitting at his desk in heaven and looking very sad. When Gabriel asks what is troubling him, God poses the question, "Does even God have to suffer?" Then, as the creator of all things sits looking even more sorrowful, a voice cries out:

> Oh, look at him! Oh, look, dey goin' to make him carry it up dat high hilll! Dey goin' to nail him to it! Oh, dat's a terrible burden for one man to carry!

At that point God stands, says "Yes," and then begins to smile as the choir breaks into a triumphant song, "Hallelujah, King Jesus."

Whether Marc Connelly, the author of *Green Pastures*, has seen correctly into the courts of heaven or not, he has pointed up the price God paid for our salvation, the rich gift which he gave to us.

And what does God ask in return? What kind of present do we give him? Some of the money which he has given us in the first place. A sharing of some of the material blessings which are ours. And remember, these are things which we use only for the time we are here on this earth. We cannot take a penny of this with us.

This is not a fair exchange of gifts. God does not look at it in that way. But we at least can show our gratitude for what our heavenly Father did for us when he gave his Son. We are not trying to pay God back for his gift. We cannot do that. But at least we can show our thankfulness.

And the interesting thing is that both gifts have the same purpose. God gave so that we might not perish but have eternal life. And the gifts we give to the church have that goal in mind too. When we share our blessings, the money received is intended to spread the good news of the gospel. The money you pledge or place in the offering plate may be the means of telling someone else the good news of the gospel. For the church exists to keep alive the message that we have a Savior who can release human beings from the chains of sin. People in the past have given so that you now know of God's goodness. Your gifts to this church will enable others to learn about Jesus Christ.

I began by talking about God giving. I want to close by talking about your giving. But I have talked enough about that too. Now it is up to you. The giving is now in your hands. In the light of John 3:16, bring your gifts.

8

Which Is Your Group?

Text: Luke 10:29-37

If I were to take a poll this morning, I'm sure this congregation would select the parable of the good Samaritan as one of its favorites. Jesus had a way of telling a story in such simple, clear language that he charmed his listeners and silenced his enemies. And the good Samaritan is an excellent example of his technique. He told the parable in response to the question, "Who is my neighbor?" and Jesus' answer seems to have settled the question for all time.

But often we don't recognize there are layers of truth and hidden meanings in the simplest parables. The church has been studying these little stories for 20 centuries and still hasn't exhausted the meanings. So I would like to show you this morning a slightly different approach to the story of the good Samaritan. I believe that in this old story Jesus gave us a picture of all humanity and also provided us with a memorable lecture on Christian stewardship. I therefore invite you to look at four groups portrayed here and to choose your own group.

Let's begin with the man who went down from Jerusalem to Jericho and fell among thieves. There wouldn't be any story without him. We can label him *the victim*. That's about all we know about him. We don't know whether he was a merchant or a traveler, a sightseer or a man who was going to visit friends or relatives. He may have been unwise or unlucky, but as we begin the story he is lying along the road, half dead. He is a poor, unfortunate individual, but he represents a large part of this world's population, the people who are the victims of life.

Walk through the slum sections of any large city and you will see them—the winos, the people high on dope, the ragged, the hungry. They all have sad stories to tell, and, whether they are telling the truth or not, these people are the victims of life.

Actually, you don't have to leave home to come in contact with life's victims. The newspapers and the TV will make you acquainted with them. Here are refugees from Afghanistan and Haiti and Southeast Asia. Here are blacks and whites, oppressed in South Africa. Here are storm and famine victims from everywhere. You can read about or see people dying on the streets of Calcutta, people being sent into exile in Russia, bomb victims in North Ireland, etc., etc.

The sad thing is that most of the victims of the world have no control over their fate. Think of the American hostages in Iran. Regardless of the right or wrong in our dealings with that unfortunate country, the hostages had little part in what had occurred. They simply were there when trouble broke out. They were there at the wrong moment. All existence is like that. Be at the wrong place when war breaks out, be at the wrong spot when a car skids on the highway, be in the wrong business when a depression comes, and you are a victim. We must not forget Jesus' parable begins with a victim. I ask you to keep that fact in mind.

Now we come to some other characters who do not actually appear on the scene but are part of it. Jesus said robbers attacked the man who is the victim in our story. Where there are victims, there are *aggressors*—people who live by the misery they create in this world. Of course some people suffer because of natural disasters such as tornadoes, drought,

115

earthquakes, etc. But much of the suffering human beings face is caused by others, by the aggressors. Robert Burns said it well: "Man's inhumanity to man makes countless thousands mourn" ("Man Was Made to Mourn"). The pages of human history are blotted with the blood of millions of innocent victims, and the aggressors never seem to care. The leaders who plot war never think of the lives disrupted, the careers destroyed, the romances blighted. The dope seller is unconcerned about what happens to his customers. Those who rob old people of their government checks never seem to care about those whom they mistreat.

The notorious bank robber, Willie Sutton, when asked why he robbed banks, simply declared: "Because that's where the money is." He didn't give any thought to those whom he had victimized by his crimes. The aggressors, the cruel ones, never do. But they are a part of the world scene. I ask you to keep the robbers in mind for a few moments.

And now we come to those two contemptuous characters, the priest and the Levite. They are the *uninvolved*. They didn't do anything evil. They robbed no one, and they didn't purposely cause any trouble. They simply passed by on the other side. I said they were contemptuous, yet at times we are inclined to envy the uninvolved. How easy to pass through life undisturbed by the troubles of others, able to ignore victim and oppressor alike. How simple to ride the subways of New York and see people being attacked and not feel any obligation to lift a finger to help.

I am reminded of a beggar who approached a rich man in his beautiful home and pleaded for some help. After hearing the sad story, the rich man rang for his butler and told him: "Throw this man out. He's breaking my heart." But the priest and the Levite didn't even have to do that. They simply walked by and failed to act.

We may be surprised that Jesus selected two religious leaders to represent the uninvolved, for these were the men you would expect to be of help. Thus Jesus makes the point that

116

often those who pretend to be religious are the ones who refuse to take the time and effort to assist others. It's so easy to be uninvolved, and our modern world has made it even easier to insulate ourselves from life's victims. Our high-speed expressways carry us past the homes of the poor, and we are unaware of their existence. Our TV news presents us with so many sad stories that we become hardened to tales of misery. In an interview, Taylor Caldwell, a popular novelist, put it very well:

> Who, for instance, except for a very few, weeps for the murdered Jews of Europe or the ten million peasants who were slaughtered by Khrushchev in the Ukraine? Who cries out against the misery of the captive nations under communism or the Berlin wall? We prefer to coexist with evil.

Coexist with evil! Those may sound like practical words, but they are not words for a Christian. The good Samaritan in our story represents the *helpers*, those who stop by the road, those who go out of their way to aid those in trouble. And the Bible makes very plain that this is the only acceptable Christian attitude.

> So then, as we have opportunity, let us do good to all men, and especially to those who are of the household of faith (Gal. 6:10).

> But if any one has the world's goods and sees his brother in need, yet closes his heart against him, how does God's love abide in him? (1 John 3:17).

The great judgment scene as described by Jesus in Matthew 25 pictures the helpers as the ones who will be received into God's kingdom. "I was hungry and you gave me food, I was thirsty and you gave me drink. . . ."

A few moments ago I put the victims on hold. Now I would like to talk about them again. They are the ones we must be concerned about. We may not be our brother's keeper, but we are everyone's brother and sister. The victims of this world need our help, and we dare not pass by on the other side. That's why I am appealing for your contributions today. Your gifts can help the victims today, just as that good Samaritan aided the stricken man along the road.

But I don't want to forget the aggressors either. Today we have a lot of proposals to deal with the criminals in our society, but we have not been very successful in our efforts. I only know of one idea that really works. It is to *change the person.* Jesus turned Zacchaeus the crooked tax collector into an honest man. He changed Saul the persecutor into Paul the great apostle. He moved people from the aggressor class into the helper designation.

No one claims the church can do this for everyone. There have always been aggressors and victims, and I suppose that situation will continue as long as this sinful world continues. But through our gifts we can do something to help bring the gospel to those who need it and to assist those who have fallen victim to life's hardships. No one says evil people must remain evil or victims must always suffer. We have the power to change things.

Our parable, then, presents us with two choices. Some of you may have suffered some losses, but few are really victims. And I hope and pray none of you must be listed among the aggressors in this world. But you can be like that priest and Levite if you wish. You can be like that by simply doing nothing. Or you can be like that godly man who stopped by the road and helped a victim. You can be a good Samaritan. I ask you to choose your group this morning and to choose wisely. And you will indicate your choice by your gifts.

9

Don't Forget the Others!

Text: 1 John 3:17-18

A young girl once asked her mother: "Is it true, what the preacher said last Sunday, that we're put in this world to help others?" The mother said the preacher's statement was correct. "Then," asked the girl, "what are the others for?"

I suppose we have all wondered about the same question. There always seem to be others needing our help. The United Way, the Salvation Army, and dozens of other organizations are always asking for funds to help those in need. The church asks us to help people starving in Ethiopia or India or a dozen other places. Everywhere we turn there seem to be others with their hands out asking for contributions. We too may wonder what the others are for.

Now don't get your hopes too high. I have no intention of saying this morning, "You've done enough. Let's all take a vacation from charitable giving and let the *others* take care of *our* needs for a while." We cannot say that as Christians, for as long as God has blessed us with the means to share with others, we must pass our blessings on to those who are less fortunate than we are.

Listen to the words of John in his first epistle:

But if any one has the world's goods and sees his brother in need, yet closes his heart against him, how does God's love

abide in him? Little children, let us not love in word or speech
but in deed and in truth (1 John 3:17-18).

It is interesting to note that James says almost exactly the
same thing in his epistle:

> If a brother or sister is ill-clad and in lack of daily food, and
> one of you says to them, "Go in peace, be warmed and filled,"
> without giving them the things needed for the body, what
> does it profit? So faith by itself, if it has no works, is dead
> (James 2:15-17).

The apostle Paul states the same truth in a positive way. He
writes to the Galatians:

> And let us not grow weary in well-doing, for in due season
> we shall reap, if we do not lose heart. So then, as we have
> opportunity, let us do good to all men, and especially to
> those who are of the household of faith (Galatians 6:9-10).

Paul showed he was not simply passing out advice, for he
raised a large sum of money from the Gentile churches to take
to the Jewish Christians in Jerusalem who were in need of
help.

Now here we are, some 1900 years later, and the situation
hasn't changed a bit. There are still people in the world today
who need our help. The world has not abolished poverty,
despite the technological advances that have been made over
the centuries. We are more successful in devising new ways
to kill our fellow creatures than we are in meeting human
needs. Jesus' statement "The poor you have with you always"
has been proven true again and again. And we who have been
blessed must be concerned about the needs of others.

I know some of you are saying this morning: "Poor people
bring their troubles on themselves. They don't manage well.
They're ignorant or lazy. They don't deserve our help." Possibly what you say is partially true. How fortunate we are not
to be bad managers or ignorant or lazy. But that doesn't re-

lieve us of our responsibility to help others. You don't let
people starve to death because they may not have as high
standards as we do. You help them and try to guide them
into better ways. Nothing is said by John or James or Paul
or Jesus about helping only those who deserve our help. The
biblical emphasis is on need and our response to that need.

John's words which I quoted a few moments ago are pre-
ceded by the statement that Christ laid down his life for us.
Did you ever think of the arguments Jesus could have used
to avoid that action? Human beings are lazy, shiftless, no
good. They have brought their troubles on themselves. Why
should I do anything to help such people? Of course our Lord
didn't say anything like that. He helped us even when we were
enemies of God.

I think we must recognize that much of our prejudice
against the poor of this world is really an effort to avoid helping those in need. Many people are caught in circumstances
they cannot avoid. Famine may strike a portion of the world.
Sickness, old age, inflation, and a dozen other problems may
reduce families to dependence on outside help. And all people
are not equal in intelligence, education, or opportunity to
work. An old Indian saying warns us: "Never judge another
man until you have walked three days in his moccasins." We
are not to sit in judgment over others. We are called to help.

You may think I am being very insistent about the need
to help the poor of this world. I am, for two very good reasons.
Of course the poor benefit from our help. But we must recognize the world measures our Christianity by the actions we
take, not by the words we speak. The church today is putting
a strong emphasis on personal witness, on willingness to testify to others about our faith. I have no intention of saying such
testimony isn't important. But it is completely nullified by our
actions if we don't follow through and help others.

Helmut Thielicke, a famous German preacher, in his book
What's Wrong with the Church?, says there is a crisis in the
church because people have begun to suspect the ministers

aren't living up to their statements from the pulpit. He puts the matter in a striking fashion by saying people are wondering if the preacher is drinking the kind of soda pop he is advertising. If church people raise that issue with the preacher, how much more do those outside the church wonder about all Christians? Do Christians really act? Are they doers of the word, or just hearers and talkers?

"What you do speaks so loudly I can't hear a thing you say!" Those words express the attitude of most people who are outside the church. They expect Christians to show love and not just talk about it. People refuse to join the church because they feel it is full of hypocrites. Although that's often an excuse, it is also a charge we cannot deny if we refuse to aid those in need. Actions are important as a witness to those who are not Christian.

But even more important, we must recognize that our concern for others is the standard God uses to measure our faith. John in his epistle is very insistent, very harsh in his judgment of those who fail to help others, particularly their Christian brethren: "How does God's love abide in him?" James uses the same kind of language saying, if we refuse to help others, "What does it profit?" Then he sums up the matter by stating: "So faith by itself, if it has no works, is dead."

Let's face it—helping others is a basic part of our Christian faith. When the church asks for money so it can try to meet the needs of those in trouble, it is doing what God wants his church to do. Of course we can't feed all the hungry people in the world or heal all the sick or lift everyone out of the poverty level. But we can try. We can show love for others by our gifts to the church.

You are probably familiar with the story of the two men who were talking about their sons. The first one said, "My son is always asking for money. I get very tired of it."

The other man replied: "My son never asks for money. You see, he's dead."

The point is clear. If the church is alive, alert, aware of the great needs of people in this world, it will ask for funds again and again. If it has no appeals to make, that's a sure sign the church is dead, no matter how many members it may claim or how many activities it may carry on for its own people. For the life of the church is measured by its concern for others, its involvement with the needs of this world.

It so happens that I am not making any special appeal this morning. But I don't want you to be misled by that. The church must always be ready to answer appeals for help. John Wesley, the founder of the Methodist Church, was once asked to give a good motto for Christians to follow. He said, "Do good and don't get tired." That's good guidance for us all.

10

The Joy of Giving

Text: Matthew 25:34-40

"Give till it hurts." We have all heard that plea used in financial appeals. It seems to be based on the notion that we all have a certain amount of excess money in our budget and it is possible to skim off that excess without our suffering any great loss. So we can give until a certain point is reached and then pain sets in. And that's the time to stop giving.

Frankly, I have nothing good to say about "Give till it hurts." One objection is that some people are so sensitive when it comes to money that they have an easily bruised pocketbook. They begin to hurt almost immediately when the subject of giving is introduced.

But more importantly, the whole idea that giving can cause pain is the reverse of the Christian message. Actually the motto should read: "Give because it feels so good when you do." Giving should be a joy, not a hardship. It is still true that the Lord loves a cheerful giver, and that statement reminds us it is possible to give and find pleasure in it. The only problem is that many Christians do not know how to give cheerfully. I would like to discuss that difficulty today.

I want to begin by calling your attention to some features of the judgment scene as recorded in the gospel of Matthew. You have all heard the basic message here. Jesus tells his disciples that when he comes in his glory, he will be seated on a throne, and all the people of the world will be gathered before him. On the right hand will be the sheep, those who will be welcomed into God's kingdom. On the left will be the goats, those who are to be rejected. And the basis of judgment is whether or not the faith of the individual has moved him or her to do works of kindness, of charity. "I was hungry and you gave me food, I was thirsty and you gave me drink, I was a stranger and you welcomed me, I was naked and you clothed me, I was sick and you visited me, I was in prison and you came to me" (Matt. 25:35-36).

We could talk a lot today about the last judgment, but the point I want to emphasize right now is the personal stress in Jesus' words. *I was* and *you did*—in every case the actions are on a one-to-one basis; they represent human beings helping other human beings. And it is here that the real joy of giving can be found—we help others who need our help. Giving, then, is an act of love, a show of concern for someone else.

We should never lose this concern for those around us. But we may not always know personally anyone who is hungry or in prison or in need of clothes. So if we are going to help people in need, we must do it through gifts to the church and to other organizations set up to distribute charity. And here is where we lose the joy of giving. We are tempted to think only in terms of a budget—so much money is needed to help handicapped children, so much must be raised to meet the benevolence program of the church, etc. In that shift from the personal to sums of money, our contact with the individual is lost and giving becomes a chore, not a joy.

What is needed, then, is a return to the sense of human beings in our giving. I don't mean that we should abolish budgets and goals, but that we must translate these items back into the personal. Let me show you what this can do. Suppose your church is appealing for money to build a new educational building. Don't think in terms of bricks and mor-

tar and plumbing—let the building committee concern itself
with such items. Think in terms of a little, curly-haired girl
or freckle-faced boy learning Bible stories in Sunday school.
Think of what it will mean to a child throughout his or her
life to have had the opportunity to learn about Jesus in that
educational building. That makes giving a joy.

Or again. Suppose your church asks for gifts for the benevolence program of the church at large and needs a certain
amount of money to meet its pledged quota. As an appeal,
that approach is not very inspiring. But think of the appeal
in terms of human lives. Some of the money raised will make
it possible for a brown-skinned woman in Madagascar or a
man in Papua New Guinea to hear about Jesus as Savior or
to be healed in a Christian hospital. Some of our gifts will
make it possible for a woman who is alone in this world to
spend her last years in a church-sponsored old folks home.
Some contributions may help a student at the seminary to
prepare for the Christian ministry and thus to serve thousands of people during a lifetime in the Lord's service.

It's unnecessary for me to go on. You see, the joy of giving
lies in other people. It lies in this one-to-one relationship
between you and the individual benefited by your gifts. We
always give to people, and although we may never meet personally those who have benefited, we need to visualize them
as human beings, children of God, individuals for whom
Christ died. That makes giving a joy.

There is a story about an invalid woman who received a
basket of fruit from a church. She sent the fruit back with
the message, "It's people I want, not things." That story can
speak to us in reverse. It's people we are giving to, not things.
The joy of giving is to be found in people.

But there is something even more wonderful in this judgment scene. Jesus uses the personal pronoun in all these pro-
nouncements: *I* was in prison, *I* was hungry, etc. And when
the sheep on his right, mystified by such a statement, ask
"When did we do this to you?" he tells them: "Truly, I say

126

to you, as you did it to one of the least of these my brethren, you did it to me" (Matt. 25:40). What a marvelous statement. What wonderful assurance. When we help others, we are actually helping Jesus.

In a legend that appears under many guises in many lands, people come in contact with another human being who needs help and who turns out to be Jesus in disguise. Sometimes people help a child in the forest and they are really helping the Christ child. Sometimes an old beggar comes to the door and is revealed as Jesus. There are sad aspects to this legend too, for at times the individual who is Jesus in disguise is turned away, and the people miss a blessing. But the basic idea in every legend is that by helping another human being we just *might* be dealing with the Savior himself.

But Jesus goes beyond all these legends. He says we are *always* helping him, that it is not a case of *possibly* helping the Lord but *actually* doing it. He makes it sweeping: "As you did it to one of the *least* of these my brethren, you did it to me." So helping to provide a Sunday school class for a three-year old is helping Jesus. Aiding an old woman to find a few years of peace at the end of life is helping Jesus. Assisting a seminarian to prepare for the ministry is aiding Jesus. Bringing physical or spiritual healing to a native of Papua New Guinea or Madagascar is bringing healing to Jesus. And that is the joy of giving.

Now suppose Jesus stood at your door this morning, arrayed in all his royal robes, and asked for food or clothing or anything else that you possessed. You know you would bustle about to provide whatever he asked for. You would count it a great privilege to be allowed to help. How could you refuse the one who gave his life for you and who still guides and helps you through all the problems of life?

But the point of Jesus' words as reported by Matthew is that Jesus *does* stand at the door and ask for your help. He's there in the person of everyone who is in need: the hungry, the poorly clothed, the prisoner, the sick—all.

And while we find no joy in others' misfortunes, we should find joy in assisting them. What a pleasure to be able to do even a little to show our love for Jesus and what he has done for us. Give till it hurts? Nonsense. Give because it feels so good when you do! That's the joy of giving.